the
pleasures
of
pattern

THE TEXTILE MUSEUM, WASHINGTON, D. C.

the pleasures of pattern

william justema

Reinhold Book Corporation

New York   Amsterdam   London

To Doris

Frontispiece. Detail from a fragment of a 16th century Persian rug with an arabesque border. (Collection of The Textile Museum, Washington, D. C.)

© Reinhold Book Corporation 1968
All rights reserved
Printed in the United States of America
Library of Congress Catalog Number 67-14156
Designed by Myron Hall III, Emilio Squeglio, and the author
Type set by Graphic Arts Typographers Inc.
Printed by Halliday Lithograph Corporation
Published by Reinhold Book Corporation
430 Park Avenue, New York, N.Y. 10022

contents

acknowledgments

This book became a reality only because it had an ardent champion in Mr. Jean Koefoed, Publisher of Trade Books, a superb editor in Mrs. Margaret Holton, and two inspired designers in Mr. Myron Hall III and Mr. Emilio Squeglio—all of the Reinhold Book Corporation.

A special note of thanks for the kindness shown me by a number of individuals appears on page 226.

fOREWORD

Modern art is the celebration of design. If the reader finds this statement self-evident he need not read the next few pages, for they are, to some extent, the synopsis of a familiar story. If, on the contrary, he questions the statement, I think that what follows will be of interest. All art, always, has depended on the elements and the devices of design for its effectiveness, but at certain times this dependence has gone unnoticed. That may be the situation at the moment. When cults are strong—whether they are cults of religion, statehood, literature, nature, or science—men are more aware of art's "subject," and its exegesis, than they are of art's purely structural and ornamental properties. It was at one of these times, quite a literary time towards the end of the last century, that Impressionism came along.

Not that Impressionism brought design out into the open. Far from it. Impressionism was design still considerably disguised under pseudo-scientific trappings. Just as the art of today makes a program out of psychological paradoxes, central to which is the proposition that advanced art is anti-art, so the vanguard painting at the close of the nineteenth century purported to analyze and depict atmospheric light. This was what we would call the Impressionist gimmick, and it was mostly studio talk. What artists proclaim and what in fact they accomplish are apt to be two different matters. Pictorial art before Impressionism had been based on the observation of nature, even in Egypt and the Far East where it was bound by rigid conventions. What was new about the Impressionists was not their theories about light, it was the way their canvases revealed to the general public, to the layman, the astounding fact that *a painting is something that is made of paint.* For the first time the medium became more important than the subject.

Who in his fifties or sixties does not remember going to painting exhibitions in his youth and being told to "stand farther back"? There we were, crossing and recrossing a room, trying to bring into focus and a coherent whole the pictures on the opposite wall. Alas! All too frequently the image, thus reassembled, was remarkable mainly for its formlessness. The painter, no Seurat, had dutifully broken his subject down into confetti-like dots and found himself unable to hold them together. Many of Impressionism's camp followers were in the same predicament. They relied upon the frame to give a picture whatever form it possessed; otherwise it could have gone on and on until someone cut off a piece.

Now this state of affairs, as we know, troubled a man named Paul Cézanne. He too enjoyed painting with soft prismatic brushstrokes ... and then got tired of it. What he wanted was to give his pictures more substance, more—as he wistfully put it—"museum" quality. To this end he evolved a system of advancing (warm) and receding (cool) colors, which would help him to attain rounded, that is to say, *modelled forms without shading,* and a structure of grid lines, indicating planes, which would support these shapes and relate them to each other. Cézanne thought of a picture primarily as an organization of these semi-architectural components; if he failed to "realize" his multiple intentions we understand that he abandoned his landscapes in the fields. On the other hand, he might require a score of sittings for the shirt-front, alone, of a portrait.

Thus far the course of modern art is almost absurdly easy to follow. Somewhat inadvertantly, Impressionism stressed the pre-eminence of pigment, of broken color, and then Cézanne set himself the formidable task of building something solid and lasting out of the pieces. He counselled painters to see in nature "the sphere, the cylinder, and the cone," which gave them the clue to seeing African sculpture (then beginning to be collected) in a light that led to Cubism. But these two sources tend to over-simplify the origin of the first truly abstract art. I see the Japanese print as making an equal contribution. Hadn't a number of one-time Impressionists been using "oriental" practices for many years? Aerial perspective, asymmetrical balance, pattern imposed on pattern, flat areas of bold color, or else color so subtle that it was hardly more than a breath, these, too, went into Cubism.

Even so, Cubism remains a unique phenomenon. Its probable sources no more explain it than lightning explains electricity. This first giant step into pure abstraction was, of course, taken, Siamese-twin fashion, by Pablo Picasso and Georges Braque. Within the space of half a decade (roughly from 1910 to 1915) they produced works of such originality, austerity, and elegance that the whole world's looking habits were changed. After centuries of regarding the fine arts as exercises in illustration, we were suddenly shown that nothing is really necessary but a satisfying surface arrangement.

Briefly, this is what may have happened. Picasso and Braque simultaneously realized that not even *paint* was required for a good picture. Cézanne, and perhaps unconsciously the Japanese printmakers (whom Picasso is said to have despised, although he owed so much to their illustrious heir Toulouse-Lautrec), having convinced them that a geometrical framework was indispensable, they proceeded to make this same framework their subject-matter. A Cubist picture, as a result, is chiefly a *composition*. It consists of lines marking off toned areas which are rather loosely referred to as "planes," for only fitfully do they suggest three-dimensional forms, and any resemblance to persons or things is incidental.

A style of such severity is naturally short lived. Caprice and the artist's urge to enrich, or at least to vary his surfaces, soon produced what we know as collage: that most typical of modern art's many techniques. Braque, who started out as a household painter-decorator, is said to have anticipated collage by painting woodgrain and other patterned textures as parts of his pictures. Then one day Picasso went further, using actual scrap materials. The important point to be noted here is that collage, although it introduced some mildly realistic illusions, served—above all else—to keep the Cubist picture decorative-looking and flat.

Meanwhile other schools of varying degrees of abstraction were being conceived in several countries. At first glance, some of them, like Expressionism, seem the antithesis of Cubism until one recognizes the same impulse toward a figured surface, albeit a brighter and more fluid one. In fact only Constructivism, Russian style, and Surrealism, made in Paris and Zurich, were serious criticisms of Cubism; the former as a reminder of Cubism's early strength and purity, the latter ignoring its plastic properties altogether in favor of poetic values.

For more than half a century these two aspects of visual art have been battling, often within the same artist. Now it looks as though this, too, is a cold war that could go on indefinitely. What interests us in the present study is how frequently the opposing sides—those who stress art's architectural qualities (the Cubists and their kin) and those who favor applied psychology (the neo-Dadists and the Surrealists)—use identical devices. Time was when you could say confidently "this is 'fine' art, *that* is 'decorative' art," and describe an emotional effort that had failed as "mere decoration." But after Abstract Expressionism, Hard Edge, Color Field painting, Pop, Op, and Minimal Art, does anyone actually believe that the distinction between the decorative and the more-than-decorative still holds? The various styles of art pass by on a conveyor belt. The first time we see something unfamiliar we are impressed by it: it's "art." After several viewings we are bored: it's "decoration," or—as an innovation—it conceivably belongs to history. Rather than try to assess art on an In and Out basis, why don't we just agree that all forms of artistic expression are equally valid *as far as they are effective.*

The breakdown of traditional painting began, as we have seen, with the collage. From that moment onwards the mania for mixed media grew until it culminated, during the late Fifties, in the assemblage, an art-form

A MASTERPIECE OF CUBISM. Still Life. Oil and pasted paper. Pablo Picasso. Ca. 1912. (The Philadelphia Museum of Art. Collection of Louise and Walter C. Arensberg.) "Within a decade . . . they (that is, Picasso and Georges Braque) produced work of such originality, austerity and elegance that the whole world's looking habits were changed."

best described as a collage of objects. Assemblage in turn has produced one hybrid of painting and sculpture after another. It is impossible to take most of these productions seriously. A store-window-display kind of skill goes into some of them, but their junk origin (and potential) is unmistakable, even when it is not flaunted. One of the compulsions of the assemblers is to employ the same material or contrivance over and over again. Then, just when some kind of order seems about to emerge, it fails to do so ... which may be shrewd, although it is scarcely profound. By multiplying objects as the spirit prompted, for a time it looked as though Assemblage would give us another Victorian era—only the glass domes were lacking—but presently what are called "primary structures" emerged from the clutter. These grow simpler and larger with every exhibition. To all appearances, the new generation of sculptors intends to keep busy rebuilding Stonehenge.

But if sculpture has avoided outright pattern-making by a return to Constructivism, contemporary painting remains fascinated by it. And with good reason. The repetition of simple markings is the art expression most common to all primitive peoples; if any single spirit pervades modern art it is its devotion to primitivism. This was not evident in the Impressionists, for they considered themselves scientific, but as their stippling technique was successively broadened by Van Gogh, Renoir, Bonnard, and so many others, it became evident that an even distribution of shapes and colors was a hallmark of the modern canvas. This particular effect, that of a surface under uniform tension, is again gaining prominence as art enters new relationships with workshops and with industry. Mechanical means of production and the use of helpers increases. One wonders if it is all a Futurist gesture—for the Italian Futurists under Marinetti, prior to the first World War, were similarly entranced by machines—or whether it presages a truly impersonal production-line art. If it does, we are ready, or almost ready. Op and "reductive" art have solemnly discovered the polka dot and the stripe; the discovery of repeating patterns is just around the corner. But some difference still remains between a patterned picture or object intended to be shown singly and a continuous pattern designed for manufacture. No special disciplining is required of one; the most exact specifications must be met by the other. There is also the past to compete with. Whereas a young painter may feel safe in ignoring the history of his craft, assuming that all he needs to know has rubbed off on him, historical patterns of all periods, while perfectly visible, do not always reveal their secrets automatically.

Hence this book about them.

OFFERED AS EVIDENCE. Repetition underlies all of the arts, on every level of seriousness, but to illustrate the increasing tendency in the "fine" arts to repeat a given motif, just short of making a pattern of it, we have selected our examples from the last twenty-five years. Above: RED VOTIVE LIGHTS. Oil on wood. Loren MacIver. 1943. (Collection, The Museum of Modern Art, New York. James Thrall Soby Fund.) Overleaf and following pages: 1, NUMBER 3. Oil on canvas. Bradley Walker Tomlin. 1953. (Collection, The Museum of Modern Art, New York. Gift of John E. Hutchins in memory of Frances E. Marder Hutchins.) 2, GRAFIAS. Synthetic polymer paint on canvas. Paul Feeley. (Photograph courtesy The Betty Parsons Gallery, New York.) 3, FOCUS. Oil on canvas. Juan Genovés. 1966. (Photograph courtesy The Marlborough-Gerson Gallery, New York.) 4, SILVER RAIN. Mark Tobey. 1964. (Photograph courtesy The Willard Gallery, New York.) 5, PROGRESSIONS. Stones and sand on board. Mary Bauermeister. 1963. (Collection, The Museum of Modern Art, New York. Mathew T. Mellon Foundation Fund.) 6, EAR. Aluminum. Tomio Miki. (Photograph courtesy Cordier & Ekstrom, New York.) 7, TABLE. Nails. Gunther Uecker. 1956. (Photograph courtesy The Howard Wise Gallery, New York.) As the foreword suggests, "the discovery of repeating patterns is just around the corner."

1

2

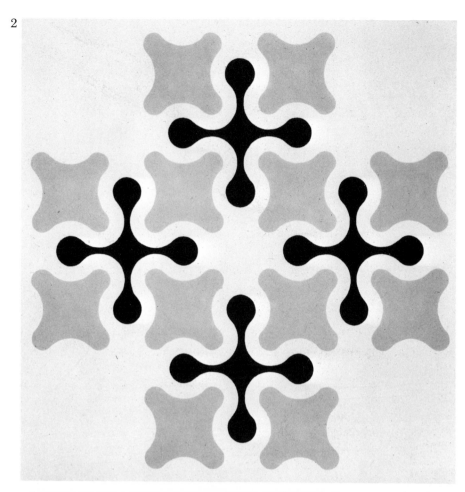

3

4

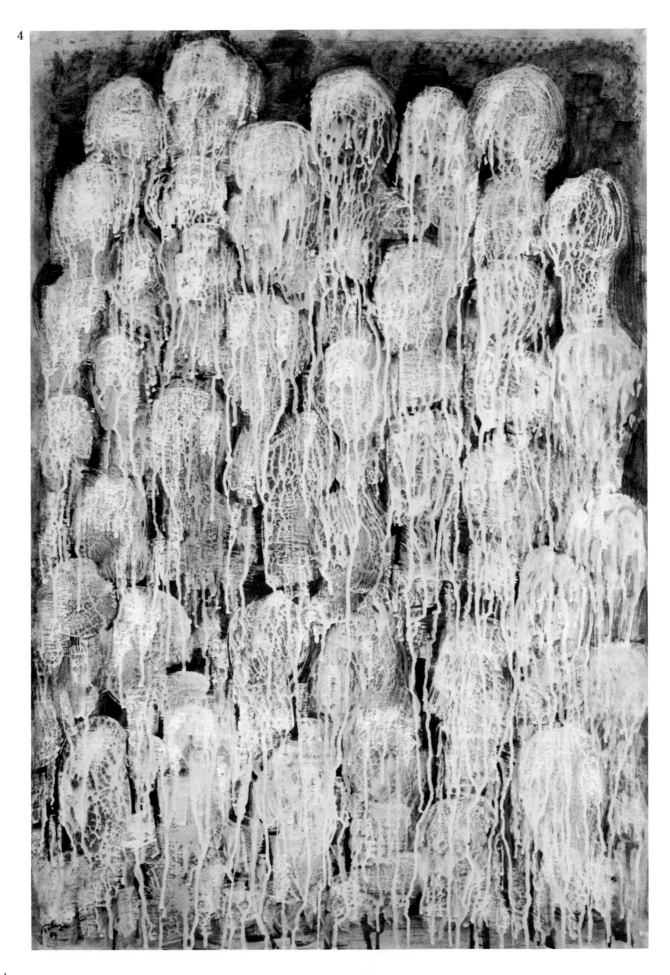

5

6

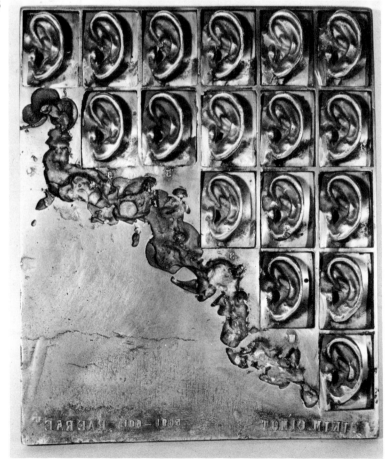

15

7

1

the
nature
of
pattern

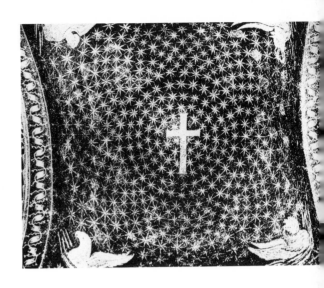

pattern in general

To dispense with formal definitions: the essence of a pattern is, quite obviously, Repetition. In the minds of many people that's all there is to it. They see a spot, a line, a shape, or an image repeated over and over and assume the result is a pattern. Well, sometimes it is, sometimes it isn't. Quasi patterns abound, and we would do well to recognize them from the start. The special pleasures of pattern are not to be experienced in poor substitutes or loose approximations, attractive as some of them are.

What passes for a pattern is apt to be on the one hand too elementary, on the other too complicated. At the extreme of simplicity, polka dots are always charming but seldom capable of sustaining our interest; they make no demands on us, which is doubtless the reason we find them charming. The old word for uniform over-all spotting was "powdering," and today such surfaces are so commonplace that professional designers refer to the smaller spottings simply as Textures. We are aware of their mass effect as we are aware of sand on the shore, leaves in a forest. But to call such rudimentary instances of repetition "patterns" is to render the whole concept of Pattern quite meaningless.

DOTS WITH A DIFFERENCE. Facing page: CHRIST AND ST. JOSEPH. Oil. Unknown painter of the Peru-Cuzco School. (In the Brooklyn Museum Collection.) Above: Center of ceiling in the famous tiny 5th century TOMB OF GALLA PLACIDIA, Ravenna, Italy. Gold and lapis-lazuli blue mosaic. Right: INFINITUDE. Oil on canvas. Yoshiaki Takase. (The Munson-Williams-Procter Institute, Utica, New York. Photograph courtesy The Mi Chou Gallery, New York City.) "Infinitude" suggests a floor pattern for a modern rotunda, a logical counterpart to the "cosmati work" on page 37.

More elaborate motifs, repeated over and over, can also appear to be patterns when they are not. Complexity alone seems to give them credence. An example of this type of quasi pattern would be a fairly naturalistic landscape framed in foliage but with the same road—or house—or wagon—showing up in the same place inexorably. It is of course possible to bring pictorial subjects into the sphere of patterns, properly-so-called, by stylizing the way they are drawn, in the manner of certain toiles de Jouy. Even so, the fact remains that pictures rarely make good patterns.

Nor do a number of separate motifs, or objects, readily add up to a real pattern. Except for being more interesting to look at than polka dots, they too constitute a form of powdering without benefit of simplicity. Sometimes these arrangements of individual items are flattered by being called "conversation pieces," but I like the term my mentor-in-wallpaper, William Katzenbach, had for them. He described most of them as "open-

PICTURES AS PATTERN. Left: Detail of Landscape with a Cottage and Haybarn. Etching. Rembrandt. Dated 1641. (The Metropolitan Museum of Art, New York. Gift of George Coe Graves, 1920. The Sylmaris Collection.) Facing page: The Four Continents. Copperplate-printed cotton designed by J. B. Huet for Oberkampf, France, Jouy. Second half of the 18th century. (The Cooper Union Museum, New York. Gift of Elinor Merrell.) The Rembrandt etching shows the basic hatching technique used for toiles de Jouy of which "The Four Continents" is a superior example, the floating-island typical of these compositions being less adrift than is usual.

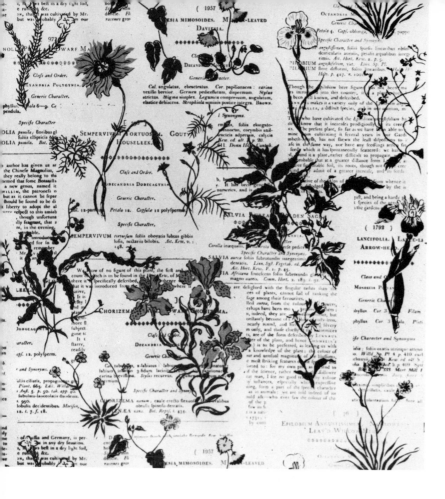

face sandwiches," whether the subject was old menus or old motor cars. This was not undue cynicism. When the components of a design retain their identity like bits of cheese, pimento, and anchovy on a round of toast, how can one fail to think of canapés?

Another questionable kind of pattern results from the use of superimposed images. Although there is excellent precedent for this from the past, where one "layer" of motifs enriches another as in a brocaded damask, today such procedure, if translated into the facile operations of silk-screen

THE CONVERSATION PIECE AND THE SUPERIMPOSED MOTIF. Facing page top: PAGES. Wallpaper designed by Zue Martin for Katzenbach and Warren. Bottom: BATTERIE DE CUISINE. Vinyl wallcovering by Piazza Prints. Above: Detail of INK BAMBOO. Painting on paper. Li K'an (Li Hsi-chai) who flourished from 1260 to 1310. (Collection: The Nelson Gallery-Atkins Museum, Kansas City, Missouri. Nelson Fund.) Both the cooking utensils and the botanical "Pages" are handled with style and restraint. As this is seldom the case, the 13th-century Chinese painting "Ink Bamboo" indicates that even quite random over-printing might be successful, provided the motifs are related and of themselves suggest such a treatment.

printing, reeks of economy and/or confusion. Certainly the intention to achieve a closely related yet varied surface through overprinting could be admirable. In that case the motifs would be designed for the purpose, not merely "doubled up" to see what happens. The use of transparent colors requires absolute control of the medium and crystal-clear intentions. Otherwise the result is bound to look amateurish.

So much for the principle of Repetition considered in some of its single, rather negative aspects. These tell only half the story, the part we wanted to get out of the way. Although Repetition is what makes a pattern a pattern, Variation is what makes it rewarding to look at, not to say tolerable! We have seen that polka dots, for instance, are generally too artless to be classed as patterns, and that, at the opposite extreme, pictorial motifs are hard to cope with because they obtrude; they insist upon being separate pictures. Variation, then, is the principle of design that relieves the starkness, spottiness, or mechanical regularity of a pattern yet holds the line against pictorial inflation.

Variation is the *intelligence* of a pattern, you could say its conscience. It gives mere Repetition those extra twists which may—possibly—make it, like the Greek Key pattern, immortal. *Together, these two principles of design can account for everything that happens in a pattern.* There is no need for us to struggle with a vague, unwieldy vocabulary. I stress a minimum and concrete terminology because flat pattern design, unlike art or the general field of design, is a very tangible subject; it contains nothing that cannot be measured, tested, verified. Accordingly we must think about pattern in the most precise language at our command.

This eliminates words like "rhythm." Repetition, with set variations, covers that situation, and without a distracting musical analogy. Even the ideas of "symmetry" and of "balance"—other textbook favorites—are perfectly easy to describe in terms of repetition and variation, as will be seen throughout the book. Why define or categorize the obvious? For good or ill, nearly everything that happens in a pattern is self-evident or soon becomes so.

If a pattern does have a secret ingredient it lies in the skill with which a pattern maker employs a few visual strategies. Predominant among these,

REPETITION AND VARIATION. Facing page: Author's sketch of a BROCADED SILK. Persian. 17th century. Right: THEATRE OF SABATA. Wall at rear of stage. North Africa. Ca. A.D. 300. The plant forms in the brocade are unusually interesting, botanically, as well as in the closeness with which they mesh. Otherwise, it is a "standard" Persian pattern with the rows of floral motifs turning alternately in opposite directions. A still more memorable instance of Repetition and Variation is the stage wall. Note the spacing of the columns, in twos and fours, the vertical fluting on some, the spiral fluting on others.

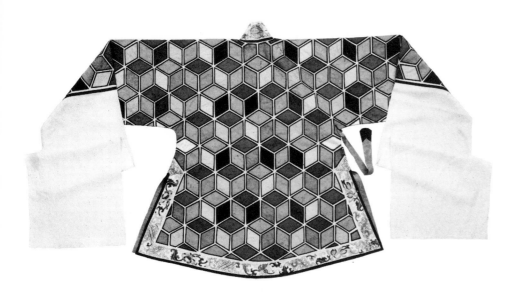

as I have said, are the principles of Repetition and Variation; these alone, acting reciprocally, can give a pattern its reason for being. Between the two of them, before our eyes, they demonstrate the nature of pattern by transforming a plain flat surface with the help of a few dots and dashes, a multiplication of shapes here, a shifting of them there. But everything, *everything*, depends on the dexterity of the designer.

It should surprise no one that pattern-making demands virtuosity. What form of art or craft does not? The earliest patterns yet discovered showed signs of ingenuity, and today, surrounded by the decorative motifs that have accrued over a span of at least six thousand years, we can unequivocally say that unless a pattern has some of the quality of a tour de force it might as well not exist. What is so marvelous about the great patterns of the past is that they never lose their power to amaze us, and then, under the right circumstances, convince us, once again, of their high degree of usefulness.

Because in the final analysis a pattern is what a pattern does, it can embarrass a given surface as well as enhance it. Although some patterns may be admired in a vacuum, for unusual merits, most patterns must be judged in context, a condition that, on the whole, is acknowledged and understood. The normal reaction to a striking pattern is the desire to see it put into action. This, however, brings up for consideration some attri-

VIRTUOSITY. Facing page: PILLAR RUG, 7′ 10″ high by 3′ 10½″ wide. Chinese. 19th century. (The Textile Museum, Washington, D. C.) Above: WOMAN'S THEATRICAL JACKET. Chinese. 19th century. (The Metropolitan Museum of Art, New York. Gift of Alan Priest, 1962.) Right: Author's PATTERN FOR WALLCOVERING. Photostat of wood-veneer collage. 1954. Charles Grant Ellis, research associate of The Textile Museum, who introduced me to pillar rugs, says they were created for cold climates and that in Tibetan lamasaries whole colonnades may be wrapped with them. The other examples of some virtuosity are variations of one theme. I call this trick "magic squares" but as it is the most familiar of all optical illusions, and a great favorite with early workers in mosaic and marquetry, it must have many names. In Colonial American patchwork it was called "Baby's Blocks."

butes of pattern beyond its two basic principles. While Repetition and Variation will continue to operate inevitably in whatever claims to be a design sequence, we now have several distinct *properties* of pattern to examine. It is a critical time. As patterns move out of the realm of abstract principles and are put to the test of performance, they invariably court danger.

Structure, the first "property" of pattern, is so much a part of *any* repeated design as virtually to describe it. You may have sensed in the discussion of some rather dubious types of pattern, above, that their chief deficiency was structural. Briefly, they were either too simple or not simple enough; they lacked subtlety and/or coherence. Maurice Grosser in his book *The Painter's Eye* speaks in praise of the "planned" picture as opposed to those which are improvised, and I can only add that, where pattern is concerned, planning is mandatory. Whether or not the plan, or Structure, is easily grasped upon viewing doesn't greatly matter. This recognition will depend (1) on the character of the pattern, (2) on the practice of the viewer. Some people learn to detect the underlying framework sooner than others, but, as you will see when we come to the section on Pattern Making, since there are only a few variations of the two basic ways that patterns can possibly be put together, none of them can conceal their construction indefinitely. My own preference is to be aware that a pattern has a strong, supple structure without wanting a diagram. Many times I purposely refrain from analyzing a pattern in order to enjoy it more sensuously.

STRUCTURE. Facing page: SILK. France. Early 19th century Empire style. Present location unknown. (Courtesy of Verlag Ernest Wasmuth, from the Renate Jacques-Ernst Flemming *Encyclopedia of Textiles.*) Right: SILK VELVET. Italian. Possibly mid-17th century. The Victoria Albert Museum, London.) These two illustrations, unlike most of those in the book, were not chosen for attractiveness but because they exemplify two extreme types of framework, one symmetrical and rigid (almost absurdly architectural for a fabric), the other fluid and "growing" (anticipating Art Nouveau).

29

With the next of pattern's properties—that of Scale—we aren't given any choice. Scale is unmistakable, inescapable. If the Scale of a pattern is right, everything is wonderful. When it is wrong, nothing seems to help. At one time we were given to understand that the "proper" scale for everything pertaining to man was the stature of man himself. And what happened? Most of us find ourselves living in cities where the public places are much too big, our own dwellings much too small. No wonder today's patterns seldom seem right for their surroundings.

Yet implicit in every pattern is its ideal size. This is something entirely apart from commercial practice or social pretension. Nor is there anything arcane about it. *The optimum size of a pattern is determined solely by the number and the complexity of its motifs.* If these, its visual contents, are limited and simple, an intimately scaled repeat may be best, since otherwise the surface will look empty. If, on the contrary, the motifs are intricate they will need elbow room, space to turn around in. Primitive man with his poor facilities for making repeated patterns could hardly err in relating their scale to his environment. Blessed are the technically disadvantaged. With every production improvement, every chance to "experiment," the tastemakers of each period find it harder to resist capriciousness.

Pattern's third property—Coverage—is so closely related to Structure and Scale that you might suppose it would take care of itself. Not at all. Whereas additions and distractions (not, please note, subtractions) might disguise a shaky structure, and some patterns, for some purposes, can be blown up or scaled down with no one the wiser, the Coverage, or *amount* of configuration in a given space, enters into a pattern from its conception. Nowadays the approved phrase for instigating a work of art is "the will to form." I would say that the "will" to cover a surface in a specific way is what triggers the designing of a pattern. A painter or a poet does not think of his work primarily in terms of subject. Rather, he feels impelled to paint in a certain style, or write in a certain mood. It is the same with pattern design. Ideas of density, delicacy, angularity, fluidity, or whatever, begin beating against the eyeballs until the designer gets down to work.

SCALE. Left: The author's wallcovering BAMBOO GROVE for Katzenbach and Warren. 1953. Facing page: EYEBRIGHT. Hand-blocked cotton by William Morris. 1853. (The Victoria & Albert Museum, London.) Where Scale has been built-into a pattern, it retains its magnitude, whatever its incidental size. The "granny" quality of "Eyebright" obviously derives from the verdure of Gothic tapestry, while my pattern, just as obviously, comes from many impressions of Far Eastern brush paintings, synthesized to make a bold stripe.

COVERAGE. Facing page bottom: A free rendering of details in the mural decoration of the TOMB OF MENA AT THEBES, 1422-1411 B.C., after a plate in *Egyptian Painting* by Arpag Mekhitarian, published by Skira. Top: FROM THE QUEEN'S BARGE. Author's rough sketch for a printed fabric, perhaps a sheer. Above: HANORA COFFEE. Screen-printed textile produced by Greef Fabrics from a sampler in the Henry Ford Museum at Dearborn, Michigan. All three illustrations are somewhat naïve. The tomb painting gets crowded with its frank delight in flashing wings, opening buds, agitated water. My own pattern, based on similar paintings, is likewise too busy. Only Hanora Coffee, who finished her sampler in 1829, kept her head while she improvised. Result: a prime example of instinctive Coverage and embellishment, down to the tail feather which continues as a vine and possibly gave Miss Coffee the notion of feathering the whole vine.

After this unreasoned start, Coverage develops quite definite implications. Heading the list is my firm conviction that a sufficiently exhaustive study of world pattern would reveal the possibility of classifying most patterns *by the manner in which the surface has been covered*. Such a study would be helpful in establishing what scholars call "provenance," or place of origin, understandably a hazardous business when the same motifs, materials, and techniques appear in objects from widely scattered places, with only guesswork as to how they got there. When we come to the second part of this section, "Patterns in particular," we can judge better whether my theory is feasible. Namely, that most periods and/or people have their own sense of spacing, and that this can go far towards identification.

But even if Coverage bogs down on what we might lightly call group analysis, it tells us much about the individual artist. To the trained eye, the rise or decline in the powers of a serious pattern designer is quite apparent in his handling of a surface. I know that coverage is to some degree dictated by the current market, yet in the very effort to meet its demands a designer will betray his strength or weakness. Along the same general lines it might be pointed out that Coverage also has a close connection with sophistication; with skill and lack of skill. How, for example, do we tell a truly naïve "document" from a pseudo-primitive pattern if both are equally crude in drawing? Easy. The document, if genuine, will be differently articulated. The motifs will be placed with some uncertainty; they won't "read" quite so well; there will be too much or too little space around some of them. In this case Coverage and Scale coincide. Both are concerned with "breathability."

And with taste. This isn't the place to go into such a slippery subject in detail, but while we are discussing Coverage and Scale it would be remiss not to mention that when these two properties of pattern go wrong, they are taste's worst offenders. Years ago the furniture and interior designer T. H. Robsjohn-Gibbings made me aware that Scale was never to be treated casually. He said that the furniture now treasured chiefly because it is "antique" was once made especially for a particular room; that everything in that room was—ideally—related to its dimensions. In this light we appreciate what vulgarities can result from scaling that is pretentious, what fussy refinements infest a scale that is inadequate. As for *surface coverage* within a real or imagined room, here we have a bit more latitude, perhaps a chance to rectify proportions beyond our control. Very possibly small broken patterns (textures, really) could be a godsend, each working a minor miracle in a designated area. Nor do these miracles need to be minor ones. Some time ago, in southern Europe, I discovered what I called "the law of profusion," which is exactly contrary to Meis van der Rohe's "Less is more." Mine says "More is less." Applied to one grandiose baroque or rococo interior after another it justifies their apparent excesses. The effects, you see, are piled on until they cancel each other out; the otherwise outrageous becomes the graciously opulent.

Pattern is always preoccupied with such matters—of too much, too little, just right. What gives pattern such fascination is that its most ordinary examples—a printed house-dress, a figured necktie—become, for everyone, an exercise in taste. People who no longer know what they like or dislike in art, feel qualified to have opinions about pattern. The assumption is that they have seen and compared a sufficient number of patterns, of all kinds, to have a basis for artistic judgment. What few people

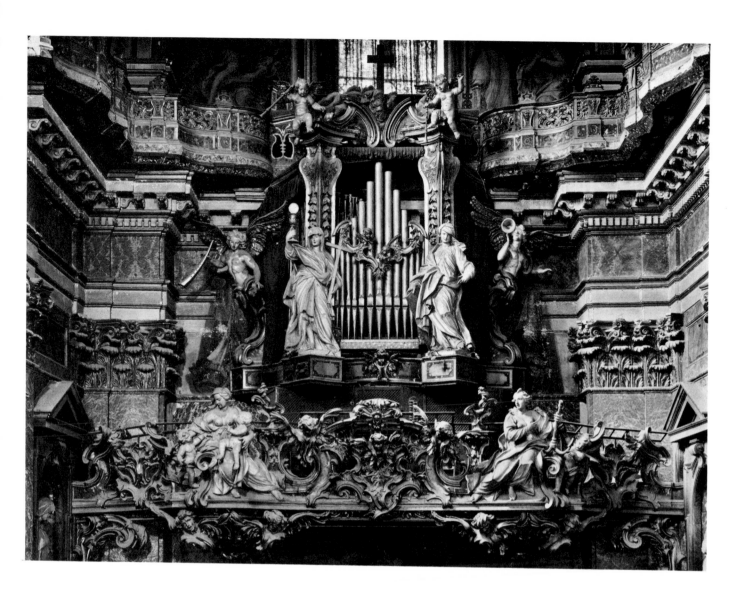

realize is the degree to which we are all influenced by novelty and surfeit. To reach objective standards of taste requires sustained effort. Some time ago decorators like Elsie de Wolfe simplified matters by referring to "suitability." I still find myself applying this rather old-fashioned test of tastefulness to patterns; somehow it keeps them on the side of common sense. For instance, to print ballroom chairs on a drapery fabric seems to me ludicrous, although I approve the logic behind the mosaic "The Unswept Floor" in the Laternan Museum in Rome, showing odds-and-ends of food—fruit peelings, fish bones—on the floor after a banquet; I merely question its discretion. But these observations touch upon specific motifs, which is the subject we will be considering next. For the moment we might conclude, with regard to a workable standard for judging patterns, that *if a pattern has any claim to excellence it lies in the relation between its size and its contents, its Scale and its Coverage.* This is as near as we can get to a visual slide-rule.

"THE LAW OF PROFUSION." Organ. Giovanni Corrado. In S. Maria Maddalena, Rome. A mad mixture of styles that is both exhilarating and endearing.

Two more terms and we are finished with our general description of what constitutes pattern. We began, as you recall, with its *principles*, Repetition and Variation. Then we scanned pattern's three *properties*, Structure, Scale, and Coverage. Between these two groups of terms we found it expedient to extol virtuosity as being indispensable to any pattern-maker, and just now we have made a few observations regarding taste, an elusive matter which nevertheless concerns everyone. These somewhat parenthetical remarks, first on the tour de force nature of pattern, second on the firm yet flexible judgment, or taste, needed to keep virtuosity under control, bear directly on our last pair of terms, Emphasis and Counterchange, the chief devices for giving a pattern the illusion of variety.

Note the word "illusion" carefully. Patterns exist for appearances, yet they are not always what they seem. In fact the best patterns, while prodigal in what they suggest, practice strict economy in the means they use. (The minimum means for the maximum effect.) Furthermore, *good patterns gain, rather than lose, by being repeated*. Not only do they disappoint monotony but the sum of their separate parts adds up, as you guessed, to a transcendent whole! If I seem a bit facetious about the entire process it is because I know, all too well, the hard work and the little heartbreaks behind it. For a pattern to exceed the sum of its parts, a con-

EMPHASIS. Facing page: Marble and colored stone Mosaic Floor. S. Clemente, Rome. Cosmati work from the 12th or13th century. Above: Cosmati. Photostat of a sketch by the author adapting the general idea of the pavement, opposite, to a repeating pattern. The problem was to de-emphasize the target-like circles (often made from a thin cross-section of an ancient column) while retaining some of the dramatic character that all large circles possess.

tinual sacrifice of treasured details must be made. Fine patterns have been purged of everything extraneous. The happy accident that can do so much for a painting is an excrescence in a pattern.

Our first new term—Emphasis—is primarily useful because it disposes of pompous words like "dominant" and "sub-dominant." I have called it a *device*, but in a sense everything that a pattern utilizes is a device. Emphasis and Counterchange just happen to be two tricks of the pattern trade that are usually not employed until after the general plan has been established. At that time, Emphasis can be invaluable. The uniform distribution of design material over a given surface, commented upon at some length in the Foreword, sometimes produces a pattern without much character: a cipher, an unintended texture. By carefully *emphasizing* this or that, by boldly eliminating whatever confuses, a pattern can become presentable again. The good offices of Emphasis are particularly notable in keeping a secondary motif in its place. This, like the sub-plot in a play, can be a terrible nuisance. It can also be an exhilarating experience. See what subsidiary motifs can do in the hands of a virtuoso designer whose "vase" rug is shown on page 60.

Counterchange—our second device—is unfortunately a technical-sounding and irreplaceable word for a phenomenon as familiar as the common checkerboard. What it actually means is "alternation," but alternation of a curiously lively kind, for it implies a sharp shifting of interest. Sometimes this shift is managed by changing the position of a single motif, sometimes by reversing the light and dark values as on a checkerboard. *With Counterchange, pattern-making started on the long road to sophistication.* Among people who are great designers, such as the Arabs and the Japanese, we find many equivocal patterns in which the "figure" and the "ground" are interchangeable, giving the highest possible degree of unity: that of identical opposites. Can one ask for a nicer device?

Our survey of patterns—in general terms—is now complete. Repetition and Variation are the *principles* that control its basic operations and demand virtuoso ability. Structure, Scale, and Coverage are the *properties* which pattern exhibits most obviously and require taste in using. Em-

COUNTERCHANGE. Left: Bookpaper. German. 16th century. Facing page: Author's simplified version of a Pattern on a Silken Cope. Syria or Egypt. Ca. a.d. 1000. Purely geometric counterchange is so commonplace that it warrants little attention. Indeed, when one is designing, counterchanges are made almost automatically. They only become interesting if a specific motif undergoes alteration, as at the left, or if, as on the facing page, leopards change their spots and birds their plumage.

ANYONE FOR CHESS? Illustration from Archibald H. Christie's *Traditional Methods of Pattern Designing* first published by Oxford: At the Clarendon Press, in 1910. (Courtesy of the Oxford University Press, New York.) Checkering appears to reach a peak of complexity in this example of counterchange. Yet the basic plan is quite simple. Mr. Christie evolved his repeat by "working an S-form into horizontal rulings and setting this pattern sideways upon itself"—beginning, that is, with a cross-banding of a single straight line with an S-curve in it. However, a close look at the pattern will reveal that each unit is composed of a square systematically extended and invaded on each of its four sides, making an interlocking jig-saw of identical shapes alternately colored light and dark. There are many ways to arrive at the same pattern.

phasis and Counterchange are the leading *devices* by which pattern is made effective. There are any number of illustrations of each of these throughout the book, all of them listed in the Index. Don't look them up until you feel inclined to. The *names* for what happens in a pattern do not matter as much as keeping your eyes open; presently the names will come to you.

Now our point of view shifts and our vocabulary becomes somewhat less technical as we make a pattern-tracking excursion into history. At times the genesis of a motif or pattern will be easy to trace, following the approved course; at other times the lack of reliable knowledge will invite speculation based on the visible evidence. What you must remember is that, under all its varied appearances and descriptions, pattern remains quite simple.

pattern in particular

When we start to consider particular patterns we are overwhelmed, at first, by their apparent diversity. This leads us to seize upon labels: places, dates, sovereigns, historical styles, craft techniques—anything to give a semblance of order and comprehension. But we soon find, if we are truly interested in pattern itself, that most of this information means very little. Once we have left behind the comfortable generalizations of the previous section, the principles, properties, and devices of pattern which might apply to almost any of the arts, we are faced with the perplexing facts of specific motifs, of subject matter. For most patterns, when we look at them closely, are made up of decorative units we would like to identify in some way. If all patterns were naturalistic and consisted of recognizable roses, or else were geometrical, composed of circles and chevrons, there would not be much of a problem. The difficulty is that many of the most fascinating patterns in the world fall, purely and simply, into neither of these two categories.

Nonetheless, the different kinds of motifs and their combinations are not as numerous as they first appear to be. I have mentioned the distinction between naturalistic and geometric subjects, and this basic division, for what it is worth, begins before recorded history and persists down to the present time. What is curious about this dividing line is its emotional implications. Everyone seems to be on one side of it or the other. Like a civil war, it divides people into two temperamentally distinct camps: those who respond, primarily, to representation in art and those who prefer the purely ornamental, which includes what we now call abstraction. It does not occur to the antagonists that realism and decoration complement each other perfectly, and that one type of expression regularly alternates with the other in popular favor. The wide gulf existing between the two schools of thought even affects scientists, who ought to be more objective. Thus, in recent times, while one group of anthropologists believed that most design motifs originated in "industry," in crafts such as mat-weaving and basketry, and hence were fundamentally geometric, another group stressed realism, seeing imitative or sympathetic "magic" in whatever form of art primitive man produced. Yet in spite of their differences as to origins, both groups, having been conditioned by academic art, on the whole agree that realism is the higher form of expression. Abstract motifs were, and are, regarded as having "degenerated" from naturalism into decoration.

Which form of art came first, no one really knows. Gene Weltfish in his book *The Origins of Art* points out that the cave artist must have had sharp tools and might well have followed up the ten-thousand-year perfecting of his flint implements with a succession of the early sculptures. we refer to as "Venuses" long before he attempted picture-making. It is true that many people who cannot draw can model or carve. What strikes me as especially strange is one of Herbert Kuhn's remarks in his *Rock Pictures in Europe*. He contends that while there were many instances of overpainting on the various cave walls, there is "no single exception to the rule that naturalistic pictures lie below, the stylized above." Does this imply retrogression or progress? People who admire illustration will say it means deterioration, people who admire design will say it marks improvement; the question of whether, by and large, decoration preceded or followed representation will remain unanswered.

But archaeology is still a young science; future diggings and Carbon I4 (the radioactive technique for establishing time with organic material, for a span of about forty-one thousand years) may have surprises in store for us. One of its greatest contributions would be the filling in of many missing links between the minor decorative arts, what one could call the household arts, and the great monuments. Man does not live by stone alone, yet unless he has told his story in stone or metal our knowledge of him is scant and uncertain. Consequently we begin our exploration of ancient patterns well aware that many clues are missing, since they were on perishable materials. The general impression one gets from the de luxe books on cave painting is that man was a pictorial artist first, a decorative artist later. And for this rather odd situation we find we can blame the weather!

Climate seems to be connected not only with preserving the vestiges of each civilization but with helping to shape it. Except for those scientists who now entertain the possibility of man's African genesis, scientists are generally agreed that man emerged, as man, around "a great inland sea" in Central Asia, and that, as this sea receded and became a dust bowl, about twelve thousand years ago, he migrated in all directions: south and west to India, Egypt, and Europe; north and east to China, and thence across the Bering Straits to the Americas. The first centers of civilization appear to have been in Mesopotamia between and around "the two rivers," the Tigris and the Euphrates; in Egypt, in China, and midway between North and South America. In Egypt, Peru, and Yucatan we have evidence of monumental building; in Mesopotamia we have mostly sculpture; in China, vessels of bronze. Only from Egypt and Peru do we have a

BEGINNINGS. Facing page: Sketch of THREE STAGES OF REALISM IN PICTORIAL CAVE ART. Spain. Approximately 40,000 to 10,000 B.C. Left: HEAD. Redrawn, as were the other figures, from *Rock Pictures in Europe* by Herbert Kuhn, published by Essential Books. This presentation may point up the fact that man was an "illustrator" before he was—as far as we know—a "designer." Even so, the more cryptic images (the darker ones on the facing page) did not, in Europe, lead to a written language, as they did in Mesopotamia, Egypt, and elsewhere.

quantity of textiles preserved in sandy, dry burial places. All these arti-facts are imposing proof of high culture, but we naturally wonder what was happening between their occurrences (the differences in time and space are staggering). Luckily, the ancient world left behind countless bits of pottery. With these we are able to put together much of the past.

What do the shards tell us? Speaking for myself, they suggest that at some stage all potters—in common with all designers—are "doodlers." Brush in hand, half their mind elsewhere, they decorate the surface be-fore them semi-automatically; with practice they become super-doodlers. I realize that this is not the approved view. Yet ever since I heard the theory that our geometrical motifs evolved from mat-weaving I have tried to estimate just how many of these virtually universal ornaments could be thus accounted for. The angular ones, obviously. It is possible to see the checkerboard, the stepped zigzag, the key meander, and even the swastika originating in plaited mats, but what about spirals, fish scales,

SUPER-DOODLING. Above: Guilloche Border. Glazed brick showing an Assyr-ian king receiving a cup from an attendant. Nimrud. 7th century B.C. (The British Museum, London.) Facing page: Jug. Iran. 1100-1000 B.C. (The Metropolitan Museum of Art. Gift of the Teheran Museum.) The guilloche border speaks for itself as an artistic invention rather than a craft by-product, and it is evident that the artist who decorated the jug did not continue to follow its outlines.

and that extremely ancient border the guilloche? Wouldn't it have been easier to "originate" some of these simply by drawing them in the sand with a pointed stick? To believe that mat-weaving or basketry produced them, we must assume that some kind of softening process took place whereby a key fret, say, turned into a spiral scroll.

Some art historians actually hold such notions, finding them more tenable than the idea of a prehistory designer with talent. A favorite explanation of the changes that occur in decorative motifs is that through continual and careless copying they evolve from one form into another. I would concede that this can happen with naturalistic motifs transported from one country to a distant one, and there misunderstood or blithely interpreted by foreign artisans. Indeed, the whole phenomena of chinoiserie is based on these circumstances. Geometric motifs are another matter. Here the concern is less with evoking exotic reveries and more with filling in spaces. It has often been observed that primitive craftsmen decorate an object—a spoon or a shield—as its shape dictates. In pottery painted with strictly geometrical motifs we see this instinct working, quite literally, to perfection. There must be thousands of clay vessels in existence, from half a dozen different cultures, which could be assigned to any one of these cultures, if judged, not by their telltale shapes, but solely by their decoration. Pottery of this quality is always very simple. If the motif is a circle it will be used with great economy. The early Italian painter Giotto reputedly demonstrated his ability by drawing a perfect freehand circle. The ancient potters were doing it all the time.

Speculation as to the immemorial origin and subsequent transformation of geometric motifs is, in any case, rather futile. When they can, scholars distinguish between "diffusion" and "independent invention," but how does one really account for the ubiquitous swastika? It turns up all over the ancient world—from China to the Russian steppes, Egypt and Peru—to all appearances simultaneously and complete. What does it signify? Everything: the sun and the cardinal directions. Nothing: the trimming for a toga. Even a slight knowledge of drawing would suggest that the swastika is an elaboration of the equally ubiquitous "Greek" key, which, at an earlier time, may have been extricated from the many supposedly ritual mazes scratched upon stones everywhere from the shores of the Mediterranean to Iceland. Or so one might romantically imagine. Where would you find a more provocative beginning than in a maze? But as Franz Boas and the anthropologists of his school make clear, while all primitive craftsmen assign meanings to the motifs they employ, few agree—even in a small group—as to what those meanings are. I strongly suspect that "meaning" is of less concern to the artist than it is to the client or the pundit, both of whom want their own kind of satisfaction. A comb-like motif was an antelope to the early Persians; it is a rain symbol among American Indians.

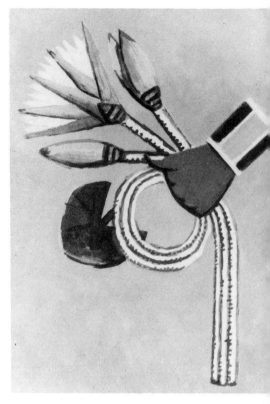

If the maze (as I merely suggest, in passing) might be called the father of *geometrical* motifs, the mother of *naturalistic* motifs is unquestionably the Egyptian lotus. William H. Goodyear, who published *The Grammar of The Lotus* in 1891, says that this flower, which he sees at the heart of nearly every ancient motif, is "not the rose-washed bloom which we now call the lotus," but the blue or white *nympheas*, "a large water-lily whose leaves lie close to the water," e.g., the Nile. In desert tombs it gives us our first flower paintings, and its use in jewelry and furniture decoration is familiar to the most casual student of Egyptian art. Needless to say, Mr. Goodyear doesn't stop here. He does a remarkable job of tracing the real flower through successive degrees of stylization in Egyptian architecture—notably in the lotiform column, at first a mere "bundle of stems"—to the completely transformed Ionic columns of Greece whose volutes, to him, are lotus petals curving backwards. Then his enthusiasm turns to fanaticism. He sees the *anthemion* (Greek for honeysuckle) and palmette motifs as lotuses seen in profile, the rosette as nothing but an open lotus seen from above. Finally, to the lotus leaf and the lotus bud he attributes the vine, the foliated scroll (the French *rinceau*), the egg-and-dart motif, and so on, while he disdains the idea that the papyrus was ever made use of; what looks like papyrus is, to him, a ribbed lotus blossom. Entertaining as this is, Goodyear's book, alas long out of print, should have raised serious doubts about tracing the evolution of *anything*. But perhaps because few people seem to have read it, the lotus cult continues.

THE LOTUS STORY. Facing page: A synthesis of THE METAMORPHOSIS OF THE LOTUS suggested by William H. Goodyear's *The Grammar of the Lotus* published by Sampson Low, Marston & Co. Above: HAND HOLDING WATER LILIES. Detail of tomb painting. Right: LOTUS CUP. Faience. Blue-green glaze with dark blue outline. New Kingdom. Ca. 1500 B.C., Egypt. (The Walter's Art Gallery, Baltimore, Maryland.)

Among other ancient flora, chief source-motifs are the palm tree, the vine, and a simple mallow-like flower which, much conventionalized, became the rosette. All of these grew in what historians call "the fertile crescent," i.e., Mesopotamia, and we are more aware of them in Assyrian and Babylonian art than we are in that of Egypt. The beginnings of the acanthus, considering the prominence it attained later, are rather obscure. A large spiky leaf was widely used for frame borders and the capitals of columns throughout the lands at the eastern end of the Mediterranean— with prodigious variety in Coptic Egypt—but I find a marked difference between these vigorous stone carvings and the delicate acanthus scrolls of Greece and Rome. Not for some centuries were leaf and flower subjects to be used as all-over repeating patterns. In classical times, geometrical, not naturalistic, motifs were favored for mosaic floors and palace walls and ceilings. This rule held for textiles, too, as we see from the garments shown on Greek vases. It took the animal world to break through into subject-type pattern.

Animal images began to appear in patterned form at least as far back as 1300 B.C., in China, on the sacrificial bronze vessels of the Shang-Yin Dynasty. These bronzes are among the great designing curiosities of all time. Reversing the usual process of natural subjects becoming stylized, theirs is a bestiary made up of odd "hooks" and partial frets, of circular mounds and squared spirals that suddenly come alive. Viewed at close range, without knowing what to look for, the handsome green-black surfaces seem to be covered with abstract figures in low relief, generously incised. Moving back, one sees something else. A strange face stares out: the t'ao-t'tieh, or heraldic animal mask. If one wishes, some of these faces can be identified as tigers by whisker shapes, or as rams or buffaloes by their horns, but for the most part they fall, like dragons, into the category of imaginary animals, starting—one might say—a long procession through the centuries. Today when animal subjects used seriously are so rare, it is important to remember that for thousands of years man lived by hunting; then, when hunting became a royal sport, animals became status symbols. As such, they entered the field of heraldry, but wherever used they commanded respect. Their realism was immaterial; if anything, composite beasts were preferred. Probably the artist-craftsman felt that chimeras and griffons were awesome subjects worthy of the labor involved.

THE T'AO-T'IEH. Left: MARBLE VASE. Honduras. (The University Museum, University of Pennsylvania, Philadelphia.) Facing page: HU (wine vessel). Bronze. China. Shang dynasty. 1766-1122 B.C. 16″ high, 11″ wide. (Collection: The Nelson Gallery-Atkins Museum, Kansas City, Missouri. Nelson Fund.) Close study of the Chinese vessel will reveal several animal masks, and it is worth noting in the vase from Central America that the squared spirals covering much of the surface also hint at faces. Squared spirals are a common form of decoration in "savage art" all over the world, but when sophisticated objects—such as these—use this motif to similar effect, it gives support to the theory that the Americas were indeed settled by migrants from China.

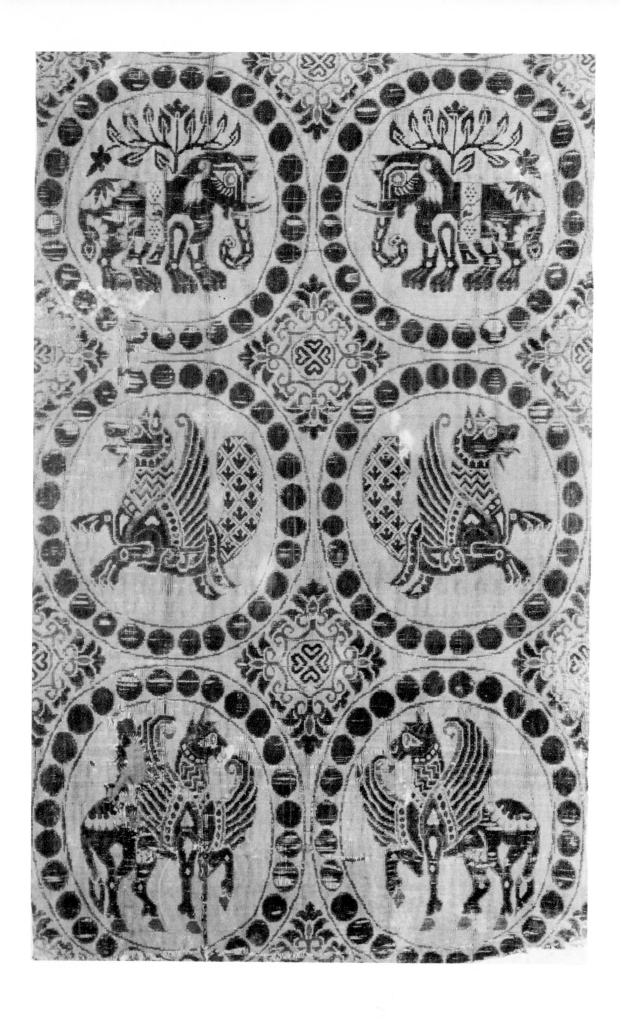

One of the earliest patterned fabrics known to exist was described in an article by John Beckwith of the Victoria & Albert Museum, "Textile Fragments from Classical Antiquity: An Important Find at Korapi, Near Athens," published in the *Illustrated London News*, January 23rd, 1954. He writes, "The design is an all-over diaper, with each lozenge containing a lion walking with tail lifted in the air and one of his forepaws raised, as if in salutation." These lions are only about half an inch high and were brocaded in fine natural linen from which the pattern thread has disappeared, leaving nothing except the holes made by the needle—a pattern of holes! The significance, for us, lies in the tentative dating, "towards the end of the fifth century B.C.," and the fact that *here we have an animal motif repeated and made into a pattern by means of a diamond framework.* It may seem a trivial matter to have put these tiny lions into "cages," but until someone had done something of the sort the great silks of Byzantium would never have been woven. Geometric motifs often provide their own structure; naturalistic motifs almost never do. Western pattern design, as an art which could make use of any and every kind of subject matter, began when it put animals into roundels.

For my taste, one or two animals in a circle are forbiddingly formal. I see them as spots that ought to be connected. Apparently the medieval Chinese felt this way too. But instead of linking together the separate

ANIMALS IN ROUNDELS. Facing page: Elephants, Hippocamps, and Winged Horses. Silk twill. Byzantine. 11th century. (The Cooper Union Museum, New York. Given by J. Pierpoint Morgan, 1902.) Above: Caparisoned Horse. Wool tapestry. Egyptian. Antinoë. 6th century. (The Cleveland Museum of Art. Purchase from the J. H. Wäde Fund.) Where and when animals were first caged will never be agreed upon. Some scholars say that the lions described by John Beckwith, above, should be assigned to 6th- or 7th-century Mesopotamia or Persia. This would make the little horse in his frame of rose-petals (derived from the "lotus" lily-pad?) an early example of enclosure, as it certainly is of naturalism. Frames such as those around the fantastic animals, facing page, are described as being of Sassanian (Persian) pearls.

GEOMETRIC AND FIGURATIVE PRE-COLUMBIAN TEXTILES IN PERU.
Above: Detail of PONCHO. Tied-and-dyed wool. Tiahuanico. A.D. 700-1100. Facing page: ACROBATIC OR REFLECTED FIGURES. Detail of wool tapestry, also from the Tiahuanaco period. (Both pieces: The Textile Museum, Washington, D. C.) Milton Sonday, Jr., former Keeper of Rugs and staff artist at The Textile Museum believes that, for the "Poncho," strips of stepped triangles were woven on a temporary "scaffold" weft, tie-dyed in various colors, separated, and then put back together patchwork fashion. The "Acrobats" are another high point in Peruvian pattern design, completely urbane in their use of light-and-dark Counterchange.

circles—made up, as a rule, of a written character or a dragon—they imposed them at rather wide intervals upon a small all-over diaper lattice usually incorporating the swastika: an effect still seen in a typical "tea-chest" paper. I'm sure the Mediterranean world was conscious of this Chinese custom, but their own pattern making went in another direction. First, they used rows of separate roundels, then rows of roundels held together by filler motifs. The last step was to arrange the roundels in staggered rows with continuously curving lines drawn, or indicated, around them. This produced the ogival framework which was to be characteristic of European patterns through the Middle Ages and the Renaissance.

In Peru the design situation was somewhat different. I understand that the exploration of this ancient civilization has barely begun, yet the evidence is already overwhelming that the Peruvians were weavers with-

out equal. A long tradition of geometrical pattern making on the loom seems to have given them the freedom to invent new techniques and types of pattern almost at will. Squares and triangles conjure up witty, and sometimes macabre, human and animal figures, while naturalistic resemblances all but vanish in the severe abstractions of tapestry weaving which appeared during the Tiahuanaco Empire, A.D. 600 to 1100. These exceptional Tiahuanaco patterns, woven as shirt material for men of rank, exhibit a contraction and expansion of their motifs according to an established plan. Ambiguous images resulting from complex planning are frequent in Peruvian patterns. A whole nation's ability to imagine and to calculate is expressed in them.

By comparison, Mediterranean patterns were simple and straightforward. On the island of Crete, before Greece came into her glory, many charming motifs were taken, like fishes, from the sea, but the only motifs the Cretans or their early neighbors, the Mycenean Greeks, developed to any degree of sophistication were variations of the spiral. Similarly, the people we habitually think of as Greek were not pattern makers. Our illustration of a repeated palmette on a small perfume flask is most

CRETE, MYCENAE, AND GREECE. Facing page: ARYBALLOS. Inscribed "Hipparchos is fair, yes." Greek (Athenian). Ca. 500 B.C. (The Metropolitan Museum of Art. Gift of Willis Bosworth. 1921.) Above: Sketch of SPIRAL PATTERN from a Mycenean dagger handle. Right: A typical SEA MOTIF found on Cretan pottery. The pattern potential of the Mediterranean islands was never realized. Its geometric decoration did not advance over that of Egypt and Babylon; the palmettes on the charming small flask are more often seen, separately, as rather clumsy space-fillers on the large pictorial vases Greece left us in such abundance.

unusual; for embellishment on their vases, they thought in terms of borders. At first these were geometrical bandings, then they were bands of stick-type Giocometti-like figures mingled with geometrics; finally they were the scenes-with-figures, synonymous, for most of us, with Greek vase painting. As sculptors and architects, the Greeks were chiefly interested in unique objects surrounded by space; it remained for their Roman conquerors to do full decorative justice to the acanthus, among other motifs, and to give it, as a branching foliated scroll, a prestige such as no other motif has ever enjoyed.

If the Greeks were primarily sculptors and architects, the Chinese were a nation of painters and poets. Craftsmen were taken for granted. Daniel Sheets Dye in *A Grammar of Chinese Lattice* asserts that the most astonishing or subtle patterns of this sort were the work of itinerant master "carpenters." Mr. Dye started collecting examples of lattice in 1916, from originals and copies of originals made between 1000 B.C. and A.D. 1900. As is evident from his hundreds of classified drawings, there is no pattern quite like a lattice pattern, either to inspire weaving or for architectural use. One can understand why the Chinese dragon didn't travel well in its original form, but the failure of the Near East and the then-West to use some of China's other motifs—along with her silk—creates one of the major gaps in pattern history. Adèle Coulin Weibel in *Two Thousand Years of Textiles* observes that "Silk brought together two great cultural spheres separated not only in space but even more in mentality: China and the Roman Empire." According to legend, silk weaving began about 2600 B.C. when the Empress Si Ling-Chi encouraged silk-worm culture and the growing of mulberry trees. By the sixth or seventh century B.C. the Chinese had set up caravan routes across Central Asia and the Gobi and Talkamakam deserts, the latter described as "the most appalling desert on the face of the earth." C. F. Hudson's *Europe & Asia* gives the fullest account of the subject I have found. He says that the Chinese alternately courted and thwarted outside trade from the beginning. Pliny, writing in the first century, makes the interesting comment that as Chinese textiles reached the west they were unravelled and rewoven in occidental designs, adding, in a footnote, "This was done at Cos." Mr. Hudson concludes, "There is no evidence that there was ever in the Roman world a taste for Chinese

CHINESE LATTICE. Left: Swastika Fretwork. The familiar tea-chest pattern in a 19th century Japanese textile. Facing page: Author's sketch of Four Lattice Motifs. Drawn from material in Daniel Sheets Dye's *A Grammar of Chinese Lattice* published by the Harvard University Press. An amazing number of lattices contain swastikas, some of them "concealed," as in the lattice used for a background on the facing page. The square of lattice at the upper right is called a "presentation" pattern in a "windwheel orientation" because it suggests the manner in which gifts were once presented, ceremoniously, with both hands; "windwheel" describes the way each unit is turned, with respect to the others. Mr. Dye refers to the lattice across the bottom as a "wave" pattern. The vertical section above it, to the left, is less poetically called "fish entrails."

CRVCIS·IACOBI·DENS·IGNATIIQ·INSVPRASCRIPTI·REQVIESCVNT·COR

patterned silk." This rejection of China's patterns continued into the Middle Ages. It was the product, not the pattern, that was wanted.

Perhaps in pique, China kept the secrets of sericulture to herself until the third century. Korea learned them first, then Japan, then India. When they did reach the Near East, classical antiquity had come to a close at Rome and the Middle Ages had been auspiciously ushered in at Constantinople. We generally think of this era as being "Christian." It was, but decked out with great oriental splendor. Josef Strzygowski, a tireless and controversial scholar who died in 1941, devoted much of his long life to tracing the Eastern origins of Christianity, going so far as to claim that many of its practices began in Mazdaism, a solar or "fire" cult based on the teachings of Zoroaster (ca. 628-551 B.C.), which flourished in early Christian times, and later, as renewed Zoroastrianism, became the state religion of Persia. Strzygowski, like William Goodyear *(The Grammar of The Lotus)*, is full of fascinating suggestions. To name but one, he submits that "The vine scroll, originating in India and Iran . . . as a purely decorative design [was] transformed beyond recognition by Rome by infusion with the acanthus, converted into the palmette in Islam, and into the lotus in Buddhist countries." For Christians it ostensibly became the True Vine ("I am the vine, you are the branches") as it can still be seen in the church of S. Clemente in Rome. Again quoting Strzygowski, "The symbolical landscapes in early Christian apses were not survivals of Greek naturalism whose 'stiffness' was due to the gold mosaic background, but were congeries of Mazdean symbols forming a composite whole. Clouds, earth, and water constitute the main subject-matter, the terrestial section being supplemented by the sun, moon, and stars." He continues, "It is admittedly impossible at present to point to a single Mazdean work of this kind . . ." but that fails to shake him. When you ride a hobby horse as hard as he, and Goodyear, did, you learn to hold on.

The above fits into the silk story because it exemplifies the fusing of East and West at Byzantium. A determined anti-classicist like Josef Strzygowski spends a lifetime trying to prove that nothing of note originated in Greece or Rome, while for us, who take motifs and patterns pretty much as we find them, all roads lead to various crossroads, and sixth century Constantinople was a major intersection. It could easily have been a cul-de-sac. Any silk for the West, whether raw or woven, now had to pass through Persia—recent routes through Afghanistan or via the Red Sea having been blocked—and had the Emperor Justinian not refused to pay the Persians the exorbitant prices demanded, sericulture might have remained an oriental monopoly indefinitely. About A.D. 550 Justinian quietly solved the problem by having certain monks from "the land of the Indians" smuggle silkworms into the empire and hatch them so that New Rome could produce silk for herself. With the Church involved, aided and abetted by a brilliant court, silk soon attained what would seem to be its greatest opulence to date. In my opinion, most of the Byzantine

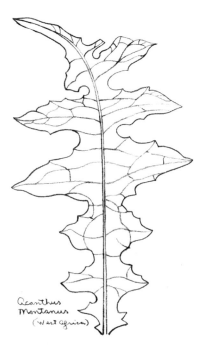

THE ACANTHUS. Facing page: Upper part of the Apse of S. Clemente, Rome. 6th century. Right: Sketch of a leaf in the Brooklyn Botanical Gardens to show the wide range of the acanthus family. Although the more classical convolutions of this motif hardly need illustrations, the reader might glance at the use William Morris made of it in the last century, page 178.

60

patterns are stiff and unpleasant, like a series of official seals, but I realize I am in the minority. As the knowledge of sericulture travelled west—to Egypt, the rest of North Africa, Spain, Sicily, and finally Italy—so did the medallion motif. This was basically the roundel we discussed some time ago, containing confronted (face to face) and addorsed (back to back) birds and animals. It is a curious commentary on both the Persians and the Neo-Romans that they kept going in circles, decorative speaking, until the Arabs arrived.

A nomad people, the Arabs had no art, no culture—nothing but poetry! Oh yes, and a brand-new religion which, in some ways, was stricter than any that had been based on the teachings of Moses, Buddha, Zoroaster, or Christ. Mohammed, the prophet of Islam (Arabic for "submission to God"), was born nearly six centuries after Christ and when he died, in A.D. 632, it took his Arab followers a scant dozen years to invade most of the fertile Near East, notably Syria and Persia. Within a century the Moslems (Arabic, again, for "those who submit") had substantially conquered Egypt, North Africa, and Spain. There are several misunderstandings about what a Moslem can or cannot do. Enrique Sardo in *Moorish Spain* says that it is a mistake to think that "the Moslem religion utterly prohibits any artistic representation of a living creature." He states that "All that is certain is that any kind of religious image is forbidden. Otherwise, there is not a single line in the Koran that supports the belief, not even in its detailed instructions." These instructions prescribe the forms which prayers, fasting, alms-giving, and the all-important pilgrimage to Mecca are to take. Beyond this there are only "injunctions" against wine, pork, gambling, usury, fraud, and slander; advice which became so thoroughly absorbed over the years that it created a climate less of prohibitions than of preferences. That this can be stronger than outright denial is worth noting. Under Semitic influence, as Sardo suggests, the Arab wanderers had merely shown a disinterest in naturalistic representation when they wove their rather barbaric-looking rugs. After settling down in Persia, the mere aversion to realism soon developed into a passionate interest in geometry, both for itself and as an aid to inventing patterns.

It is salutary that the Arabian compulsion to divide space geometrically was nurtured on Persian soil. From the days of her great kings, Cyrus and Darius, the artists of Persia had displayed a gift for sharp observation; their wounded animals in low relief, their long lines of tribute-bearers climbing the stone staircases at Persepolis step by step with the visitor

PERSIAN GENIUS. Facing page: Kirman Rug of the Vase Type. Persia. 17th century. (In the W. A. Clark Collection of the Corcoran Gallery of Art, Washington, D. C.) Right: Tribute Bearer. Author's sketch of a sculptured figure on the staircase at Persepolis. Ca. 5th century B.C. These pictures could be subtitled "before and after the Arabs." The naturalistic appeal of the early "Tribute Bearer" needs no comment. As an example of post-Arab Persian arabesque, I have chosen a notable rug. Charles Grant Ellis, Research Associate of the Textile Museum at Washington, wrote me as follows: "My feeling about this rug is that it is one of the most charming and beautiful Persian rugs in existence. I say this despite the lack of balance in its layout, which must have been designed to fit a specific purpose." He goes on to say that Arthur Pope in his six volume *Survey of Persian Art* considers it "a variety of throne rug," made for an area leading to the throne. Ellis notes, moreover, that "this is not a vase rug in the strict sense, as it has neither vase forms nor the intricate triple ogival latticing characteristic of the class"; instead, "The vine scrolls culminate in pairs of sweeping lancet forms which encircle or enclose palmette forms."

ARABESQUE, EAST. Lacquer Cup. Chinese. Late Chou
Dynasty. 5th-3rd century B.C. (Collection: The Nelson
Gallery-Atkins Museum, Kansas City, Missouri. Nelson
Fund.) Here are the squared spirals and hook shapes of the
ceremonial bronze on page 49 in a still earlier, more attenu-
ated version. We are looking down into the cup. For delicacy of arabesque, compare with the Venetian cut-velvet
fabrics called *ferronerie,* page 71.

ARABESQUE, WEST. THE SIXTH KNOT. Anonymous Milanese engraving. Attributed to Leonardo da Vinci. Ca. 1490. One of three known impressions. (Museum of Art, the Rhode Island School of Design.) As this engraving was copied by Albrecht Dürer, it is possible that it added to the fund of Central European arabesque referred to as "strap-work."

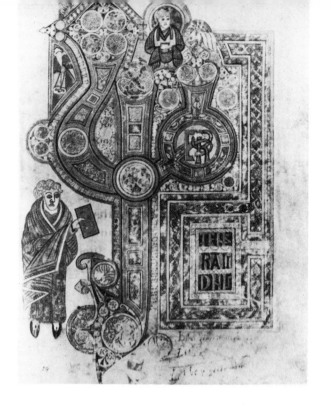

are as stirring, as delightful, as one could wish. For some centuries the Persians had excelled as warriors and had ruled over much of the known world; afterwards, like Voltaire's Candide, they were content to tend their gardens. That is what they were doing when the Arabs conquered them. Coming from desert wastes, their new masters had never seen such gardens. Eventually, Arabs and Persians, having painfully grown accustomed to each other's ways, were making beautiful faience mosaics together. These, a perfect balance of geometrical curves and floral details, embody what came to be known as arab-esques, the most spectacular of which still curl over the blue domes at Isphahan. One cannot say that Islamic Persia invented the arabesque—for the Chinese had used networks of curved lines on their pottery centuries before, and it might also be said that the acanthus scrolls of the Romans had anticipated it—but only Islam seems to have perceived the arabesque as a structural device capable of myriad uses.

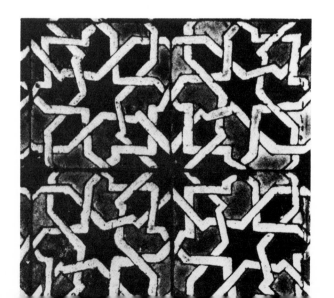

ARABESQUE, NORTH AND SOUTH, CURVED AND ANGULAR. Above: Initial and the opening words of the St. Matthew gospel from *The Book of Kells*. Irish. Late 8th or early 9th century. Facing page: "Spiral" page from *The Book of Durrow*. Irish. (Both illustrations courtesy of Trinity College Library, Dublin.) Left: GLAZED TILES. Moorish Spain. Second half of the 15th century. (The Victoria & Albert Museum, London.) The story of the arabesque is nearly interminable, but these three pictures show the relation of Celtic ornament to some that we have already seen from the near and far East. The page from *The Book of Durrow* is called "a carpet page," and the Moorish tiles (four make up a unit) are a good, if very simple, example of geometric *laceria,* based on diagonal lines forming star shapes.

Before the Arabs came the Persians had arranged their floral motifs in straight lines, sometimes turning alternate lines in opposite directions for variety. To the Arabs this was an unthinkable thing to do. If art was to be a worthy form of worship (and to the Moslem mind everything praises Allah) it must propose, and solve, new problems. Exactly what the Arabs contributed to Persian art can best be gathered, at first, from the patterned brickwork on buildings dating from the tenth century. We are repeatedly told that the Arabs were "not builders," although André Godard in *The Art of Iran* says that "they became architects"—surely a nice distinction. Before anything else, however, they were contrivers of pattern, and Lewis F. Day, a late follower of William Morris, has this to say in his nearly unobtainable book *Pattern Design:* "It is an Eastern practice (I have been told by Sir Caspar Purdon Clark) to design on the lines of a sheet of paper folded in parallel lines, and folded again at right angles to those, and then again in a diagonal direction—a practice which one ought to have devined from the nature of the patterns deriving from it." Mr. Day is referring of course to a grid, which, crossed by diagonals, forms the series of intricate star shapes everywhere identified with Islamic design. We see these in abundance in Iran, but in fairness to Persian genius it should be said that once the Arabs had given them the arabesque, their use of it, particularly in the rugs they wove, became triumphantly their own. By this time the spirit of Islam had moved on.

Was the Arab seeking new gardens? He found them in Spain. Furthermore, here he found an identity which had been denied him in Near Eastern countries. The phenomenon is not unfamiliar. A man leaves home, and draws nearer to his origins than he ever was before. The Arabs, during their eight centuries in Spain, from 711 to 1492, could be regarded as the answer to the art historian's prayer: a group of people with a distinctive style moving to comparatively isolated, comparatively virgin territory and working out their own artistic destiny. Granted that the Gauls and the Visigoths preceded them, the civilization that the Arabs from Syria and the Moors from North Africa supplanted in Spain might be called lingering Roman or standard Mediterranean. Once again Islam acted as a catalyst. Far removed, now, from soft Persian influences, the workers in stucco, tile, and stone, in three great cities—Cordoba, Seville, and Granada—devised and elaborated a completely masculine type of arabesque: the *laceria,* or "carpentry of knots." This is a network in which straight lines predominate; the "knots" are square interlacings. Laceria, like curvilinear Persian-born arabesque, is accompanied by passages of the two types of Arabic script: the Kufic, or formal and upright, and the Nashi, which is informal and cursive; also by floral elements which are now reduced to severely conventionalized leaves known as *attawriq.* Combinations of these three types of patterning, deeply carved in hard plaster (that is, stucco) and painted with strong colors—red, blue, green, and gold—frequently covered whole walls in Spanish mosques and palaces.

Arabesque was not confined to the Islamic world; before the Middle Ages were over every part of Europe had evolved its own distinct style of interlace. I had long felt there was a connection between Eastern arabesque and Celtic illumination but until recently I would have hesitated to state it in writing. Now James Johnson Sweeney in his Introduction to an Enesco paperback, *Irish Illuminated Manuscripts,* says, "There must be a direct connection between early Irish Christianity and the monasteries of Egypt, as well as the highly orientalized Christianity of the southeast Mediterranean." That satisfies me. Monasticism was introduced into Ireland in the sixth century, roughly a hundred years after St. Pachomius organized the first cenobic community in Egypt. Coptic and Syrian monks used borders of interlace in their books and some of these doubtless reached Ireland or were seen by Irish monks who travelled south. Mr. Sweeney and other scholars carefully remind us that these border ornaments may be related to Roman mosaic pavements—of which there were numerous examples throughout western Europe—but they speak, too, of "carpet" pages in the seventh century Irish *Book of Durrow* and it seems likely that by the time the more famous *Book of Kells* was produced, during the late eighth and early ninth century, Islam *could* have made a contribution to its sumptuous pages. And why not? In perfecting the arabesque the Moslems made it available to everyone. The Irish missionaries who went into central Europe to preach the gospel might have born tidings of the arabesque as well. Whereas the monks at home in Ireland had twisted Roman or Islamic geometrical figures into fluid, burgeoning organisms, Teutonic artists restored some of their severity, as iron "strapwork," while the Scandinavian form of arabesque, intertwined with animals, goes back to the Vikings. These are only a few of the regional forms the arabesque took during the much-maligned "dark ages." When the arabesque reappears it will be as "gothic tracery"—a line-scheme shorn of much of its geometry, with living sap seeming to flow through it.

You have continued to notice, I trust, that nature and geometry remain our poles of reference. Whatever else it does, decorative art swings between them so persistently that people devoted to one or the other periodically attempt to explain the whole designing process in terms of either abstract or naturalistic revelation. We saw how absurd this became with the lotus, a motif that simply ran amok. A currently active nuisance is the so-called "Tree of Life"; it can make a satisfying study of central and south-Asian art all but impossible. This "tree," as I've watched it grow, sprang up in Assyria as little more than a stick flanked by two heraldic beasts. Before long, it flourished. In Babylonian times, ornate fan shapes, suggesting ceremonial props for a Biblical spectacle, went up one side of a "trunk" and down the other. Would this be the Sacred Tree motif, the *houma*, from ancient Persia? If so, the palmettes seemingly connected by flowing water make it both distinctive and esoteric. We know that the Greeks had their sacred groves, that in India trees sometimes "married," and that today trees are so scarce in parts of western Asia that travellers tie a rag on them and make a wish. But to call every upright flowering branch in a painted or printed cotton from India a "Tree of Life" is to parody scholarship and make the whole idea of symbolism distasteful.

THE "TREE OF LIFE." Author's sketch of the most likely historical candidate, made from a 7th century B.C. Assyrian bas-relief in the British Museum.

"Pomegranate-type pattern" is another label that means nothing. Or rather, it does not mean what it says. A few pages back, in discussing the evolution of naturalistic motifs into typical occidental repeating patterns, I briefly mentioned the ogival framework, which resulted from staggered roundels with drawn—or implied—undulating lines around them. This, the perennial "ogee" repeat, is simply a system of interlocking ovals slightly pointed at top and bottom like old-fashioned Christmas-tree ornaments. Whether the ogee was much used in Europe before the Gothic era (1150-1450) is hard to say. It is the more expensive silks from Byzantium that have been preserved, and they, of course, featured a royal menagerie in separate cages. Then Islam conquered that particular part of the world and the animals were scattered. When Gothic patterns came along several

POMEGRANATES, REAL AND SO-CALLED. Facing page: WALLPAPER. 1509. Discovered at Christ's College, Cambridge. Right: PORTRAIT OF A CONDOTTIERE. Giovanni Bellini. (1430-1516). (The National Gallery of Art, Washington, D. C. Samuel H. Kress Collection. 1939.) The wallpaper, which is the earliest known fragment of European wallpaper, shows the architectural pomegranate motif whose distinctive shape suggests the ogival repeat (see diagram, page 122), although I do not think that this particular motif used such a repeat; more probably the pomegranates, printed by letter-press on small sheets, were matched side by side in rows. The pattern in the gold-brocaded garment of the gentleman at the right—even though the fruit within its leaves is clearly a pineapple—would also, because of its construction, be classed as a pomegranate pattern.

centuries later they were simpler both in plan and subject. They consisted mostly of small leaf sprigs neatly dovetailed; of garlands held together with crowns; or, most strikingly of all, were nothing but a rosette or palmette outline suggesting delicately wrought iron and hence called *ferronerie*. With the Renaissance in full swing the ogival plan became still more useful; the rich, varied motifs recovered from classical antiquity needed a strong, pliant scaffold. What this interlocking repeat was called during the Renaissance is difficult to ascertain. In the nineteenth century a clerk hit upon the term "pomegranate" and everyone adopted the designation. But just what does it refer to? A motif, or a repeat? Over the four or five centuries under discussion real pomegranates do appear in patterns quite often, but not necessarily in pomegranate-shaped compartments. What we usually find, at the center of these, is a hybrid fruit-and-flower motif that could just as well or better be called a thistle, pine cone, or artichoke: botany was not a designer's strong point in those days. All he required was a core, or focal point, around which he could arrange his acanthus leaves. Since these were equally unreal to him, the more ambiguous the center was, the better. The term "pomme," used in France, has been suggested as a substitute, but since we are not referring to an apple, either, I think that, too, would be misleading. We should describe the subject as concisely as possible, as a fruit, floral, or palmette "core," in an ogival or simply "ogee" repeat.

Describing semi-naturalistic patterns is always an ungrateful job, so it is pleasant to turn to a group of brocaded silks in which the subject predominates. The secrets of sericulture had finally reached Italy about A.D. 1200. Lucca, a city famous for her woolen textiles, soon become famous for her silks. There was nothing quite like them. Botticelli had not

FERRONNERIE. Left: PORTRAIT OF A MAN. Panel. Probably North Italian School, 15th century. (The National Gallery of Art, Washington, D. C. Samuel H. Kress Collection.) Facing page: CUT VOIDED SILK VELVET. Italian. 15th century. (The Philadelphia Museum of Art.) In spite of their delicacy and the fact that they belong to a special group of patterns named for their resemblance to wrought iron, the patterns on both these pages might be called "pomegranate"—with the excuse that the inner shape is pointed and crested.

been born when Lucchese silks struck their fantastic stride early in the fourteenth century—midway between the Gothic era and the Renaissance —otherwise one could say that they blended Aesop with Botticelli and premonitions of Surrealism. Considered strictly as patterns, they are not too successful: the coverage is spotty, the shapes are poorly integrated. In spite of, or perhaps partly because of, this, they radiate an immense vitality. To repeat what I said at the beginning of this section, "Pictures rarely make good patterns," but—now and again—pictorial elements prove irresistible, as when they show a face at the roots of a tree, or dogs out boating! The Lucca silks are also full of strange flying animals (a Chinese influence, for Genghis Khan had again opened the overland trade routes), but what gives these patterns their signature is the glittering rays that stream from the motifs as if they were ablaze or had been sanctified. That's what made me think of Botticelli. Fabric patterns comparable to these fourteenth-century silks, woven, primarily, at Lucca, were not to occur again for several hundred years and then under the most mysterious circumstances.

Meanwhile, contemporary with them or slightly earlier, a different and entirely geometrical magic had appeared in the patterns made by the Cosmati family. Their medium was not woven cloth but pieces of colored marble and stone. You can see "cosmati work" on the floors of half the old

LUCCA, ITALY, EARLY 14TH CENTURY. Facing page: Detail of a BROCADED SILK. (The State Museums, Berlin.) Above left: The same pattern in repeat. Above right: Fragment of another Lucchese silk. (The Textile Museum, Krefeld, Germany.)

churches in Italy. In S. Marco alone, at Venice, there must be two hundred patterns, each like a small rectangular rug. Cosmati work in the form of delicate jewel-like inlay using bits of mosaic glass also decorates some dozen major pulpits and thousands of little twisted stone columns (grouped in pairs but no two exactly alike) in a score of great cloisters throughout Italy and Sicily. This type of patterning, based in architecture, pervaded the pageantry of the period, as can be seen in Uccello's "The Battle of San Romano" and, to this day, in the uniforms Michelangelo designed for the Swiss guards at the Vatican. German armour shared the same carnival qualities. Howard L. Blackmore in *Arms and Armour* writes, "By the middle of the sixteenth century there was a considerable vogue in parade armours, elaborately decorated with embossed foliage, grotesques and classical scenes." His conclusion is inevitable: that "all these fantastic garnitures, while bearing witness to the skill of the craftsmen concerned, was little more than fancy dress." But was not the whole Renaissance a masquerade, part secular, part religious? A. D. F. Hamlin in his two-volume *A History of Ornament* asserts that "nearly all the 15th-century brocades and velvets betray their Oriental origins. Even before the 15th century the Italian—especially the Venetian—painters had been accustomed to dress the Madonna in robes figured with Oriental patterns." Mr. Hamlin then cites a pattern on the Madonna's robe in a painting by Carlo Crivelli in the National Gallery, London, as "exceptional in owing nothing to Oriental suggestion," but notes that Crivelli is on record as designing some of the patterns himself. Gentile Bellini, on the other hand, was sent to Constantinople by the city-state of Venice, in 1479. He remained there for some time, painting semi-officially, and since he too did some pattern designing it is possible that he helped to popularize the new diagonal layout. Although this did not eliminate the strictly symmetrical ogee, it did provide a change and a fresh, always welcome reminder of the Orient.

The Renaissance was the time of Vasco de Gama (ca. 1460-1525) and the opening of direct sea trade with India and the Far East, pioneered by the Portuguese in the sixteenth century and developed from about 1600 onwards by the "East India Companies" of the Dutch, English, French, and Danes in that order of importance. Their main object was to bring spices directly to Western Europe and to reap for themselves the enormous profits exacted by those monopolizing the overland route. But soon Europe was flooded with spices, and so the traders turned to patterned fabrics and porcelain as more profitable merchandise. This part of the story still remains to be told in full, and, as far as patterned fabrics

LATE GOTHIC PATTERNS. Facing page: THE ARCHANGEL GABRIEL. Wood panel. Masolino da Panicale. Florentine. 1384-ca.1435. (The National Gallery of Art, Washington, D. C. Samuel H. Kress Collection.) Right: SUIT OF ARMOUR. Author's sketch of embossed armour from Bavaria, after a picture in Howard L. Blackmore's *Arms and Armour*, a Dutton Vista Picturebook. The Archangel wears a dress patterned diagonally to give a forward movement. Unless made into church vestments, few fabrics from this period survive; it is fortunate that we have painted "likenesses" of so many, as well as the ornamentation on the less-perishable armour.

"*DAMASK TYPE.*" Above: PIECE, WOVEN SILK. Italy. 16th century. (The Metropolitan Museum of Art, New York. Gift of the United Piece Dye Works. 1936.) Facing page: MERCERIZED COTTON DAMASK woven by the Gainsborough Silk Company, Sudbury, England, for newly decorated rooms at The National Gallery, London. The vertical repeat of the pattern above is eighteen inches at most; the repeat, facing page, measures more than six feet. But quite aside from their dimensions (and a few similar shapes), the patterns are almost as different as they can be and still fall into the category the trade loosely calls "damask." That is, the linear purity of the Italian silk is impeccable, while the modern fabric—although its large scale and many subtle self-toned colorings fill the role required of it admirably—has unquestionably undergone much change. Mr. Franco Scalamandré explained it this way: "Jacquard cards get mixed up or lost, now and then, and the weavers put in their own ideas."

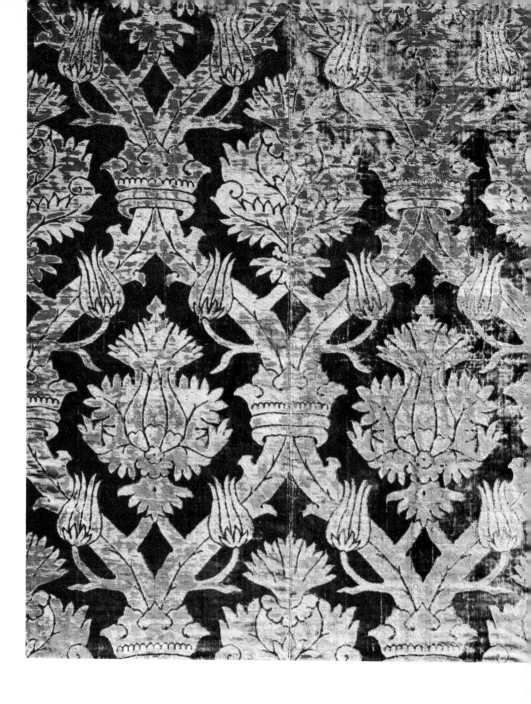

"DAMASKS," continued. Facing page upper left: Fragment of SILK PLAIN COM-
POUND CLOTH. Italian. 16th century. (The Philadelphia Museum of Art.) Upper
right: ARMORIAL DAMASK. Italian or Spanish. Late 16th century. (The Metropolitan
Museum of Art. Rogers Fund. 1919.) Lower left: PIECE, WOVEN SILK. Italy. 16th
century. (The Metropolitan Museum of Art. Rogers Fund. 1920.) Lower right:
DAMASK. "Probably Spanish." End of the 16th century. (Courtesy, Museum of Fine
Arts, Boston. Gift of Denman W. Ross) Above: VELVET BROCADE. Turkish under Italian influence. 16th century. (The Victoria & Albert Museum, London.) There is seldom
enough evidence to allow anyone to generalize convincingly about the essential
difference between Italian and Spanish patterns of the Renaissance, but it is instructive to compare the two upper patterns, opposite, and observe that the more severe
one, on the right, is thought by some (Weibel among others) to be Spanish, while
the other border-line example, lower right, has a boldness which marks it as "probably Spanish." Does a certain severity and heaviness make the difference? The
velvet brocade, above, is a "damask" of another manufacture—although all five
textiles are assigned to the same century, and all except the one at the lower left
utilize the ogival framework. What makes the Turkish pattern intriguing is its blend
of exoticism and Gothic, complete with little medieval crowns where the stems come
together.

ORIENTALISM. Above: Crewel Work, English Embroidery. 17th century. (Courtesy, Museum of Fine Arts, Boston. Gift of Mrs. Samuel Cabot.) Facing page: Printed Cotton. France. 1785-1790. Style of Pillement. (The Cooper Union Museum, New York.) Chinoiserie, as a whole, can be attributed to the voyages of Europeans to India and the Far East beginning in the late 16th century. The resulting exchange of decorative ideas infinitely enlivened the design picture—occasionally to the point of utter confusion. But two factors can usually be separated: the techniques and the subject matter. For example, the habit of embellishing a motif with extraneous, purely ornamental elements was—or soon became—so characteristic of Indian "chintz" that, whether or not other countries had used the device earlier, and independently, the effect it gives is distinctly oriental. Similarly, with the landscape subject. While many peoples made use of small scenes for decoration, circumstances suggest that the bits of scenery on Chinese porcelains were a major inspiration for toiles de Jouy, the French adding classical mythology and local color.

are concerned, it will be done in a forthcoming book by John Irwin and Betty Brett, of the Victoria & Albert Museum, London, and the Royal Ontario Museum, Toronto, respectively. Since I myself touch on the perennial taste for the exotic elsewhere, in a different connection, it will suffice to say here that Mr. Irwin has found East-West influences to be highly reciprocal. Not long ago when business men in Madras, India, complained that their native plaids were being copied in the west he pointed out that Scotland is where the patterns came from.

Trade with China had already been going on—or off-and-on—for so long that, although it was farther away than India, Western Europe was better acquainted with what it had to offer. There was consequently a seventeenth-eighteenth century style, in several phases, each accurately-enough called chinoiserie, but the English appear to have been the first to take native Indian decoration in hand and style it for home comsumption. English crewel embroidery and the East Indian painted cottons known as *palampores* were freely exchanging motifs at the end of the seventeenth century, whereas it was not until the nineteenth century that the introduction of the Kashmir shawl brought the Persian pine-cone motif (which we call "paisley" after the city in Scotland that wove imitation Kashmir shawls) to the attention of fashionable Europe. France was instrumental in this. A late comer, France assumed the position of style arbiter, of fashion oracle, early in the eighteenth century. Up until then, Italy, Spain, and Germany, in Europe, and Persia, India, and Turkey, in Asia, had shared weaving honors rather casually. Then the English, at Spitalfields, outside London, and the French, at Lyons and Tours, entered into grim competition—the former immeasurably aided by Huguenot weavers forced to leave Catholic France. The manufacturing intrigues of the period, as recounted by Peter Thornton in *Baroque and Rococo Silks*, are of interest equal to the luxurious fabrics. These are truly an embarrassment of riches, Byzantium all over again. Centuries of received motifs and manual skill went into their making, with the result that they seem to set a standard of taste which, in fact, they abrogate. I am increasingly convinced that, just as climate conspired to save some of man's first patterns for us, wealth, in turn, took over the job and for a long time now has been fostering and preserving chiefly the expensive. It is our loss. Every culture has at least two creative levels, and the more humble products of the past, following older traditions, often appear to have been superior. Or is this unhistorical romancing? The poor we always have with us and they may always have preferred poor imitations.

Except, perhaps, in Japan. This country, with a reputation for being the world's most confirmed imitator and producer of gimcracks, is nevertheless the only country that has a genuine cult of simplicity. The art of the Japanese is based on negation. If this gives them a fatal ease in copying and in shoddy mass production, it likewise gives them a peerless grasp of design essentials. No occidental can follow all the vagaries of Japanese taste, but its mastery of pattern makes that of Islam seem pedestrian,

NATURALISM. Facing page top: ENGLISH SILK DESIGN. Style of Jean Revel. Signed "Anna Maria Garthwaite," dated 1735. (The Victoria & Albert Museum, London.) Bottom: A STILL LIFE. Silk by Philippe de Lasalle for Camille Pernon et Cie. France. Lyons. Ca. 1770. (The Metropolitan Museum of Art, New York. Rogers Fund, 1938.) If some people feel that pattern design reached its zenith in extreme naturalism, those who value design, as such, feel that it descended to its nadir. The man most responsible for this decline appears to have been Jean Revel, born in the silk-weaving city of Lyons, in 1684. Revel, who gave up a career as a painter to become a designer, introduced a system of weaving called *pointes rentrés* which consisted of mingling adjacent colors to produce shading. Since no actual silks can be assigned to Revel with certainty, I have chosen, as typical, a design by Anna Maria Garthwaite, of Spitalfields, who came under his influence for a time. However, Philippe de Lasalle was the leader of the many painter-designers who followed Revel's realism. His "pictures in silk" epitomize wasted talent.

and the French, by comparison, talented novices. Like the French, however, the Japanese developed their flair for pattern through a preoccupation with costume. Back in the tenth century Lady Murasaki in *The Tale of Genji* gave us a picture of what must have been the most clothes-conscious court that ever existed, and J. Hillier's *The Japanese Print* speaks glowingly of the seventeenth century when Japan's "greatest artists were engaged to draw kimono patterns." He says, moreover, that "The subject of any print was always partly the cut of the clothes and the decorative patterns of the fabrics," and I have recently seen a sample book of pattern designs from which nineteenth-century Japanese woodblock cutters could select motifs for the kimonos to be shown on the artist's figures. When they first appeared, Japanese prints were, in fact, little more than fashion plates depicting famous geishas and actors to enhance their popular appeal. The kimono, with its wide flat surfaces, was ideal for the display of pattern; the clothes of few other countries have provided such an excellent showcase. Not content with using a single motif repeated all over, or a patterned material combined with a plain one, the Japanese, with unparalleled virtuosity, often use several types of pattern in close juxtaposition in one garment, employing a variety of techniques—tie-dye, patchwork, paint, appliqué, and embroidery—in doing so. Now and then other people have mixed patterns and techniques, but never with the same degree of sensitivity. Even if they had possessed such sensitivity, few cultures would have a sufficiently wide range of patterns to work with. For many centuries Japan created two vast stockpiles: one of geometrical, one of naturalistic patterns. What makes her contribution to design unique is the astonishing way she welds them, finding subtle affinities under totally different appearances.

Returning to Europe, via the Near East, we discover that Chinese motifs, no longer ignored, permeate the whole civilized world. The dragon, in many degrees of abstraction, is a feature of rugs from the Caucasus, cloud bands are a staple of Persian rugs and painted miniatures, while the

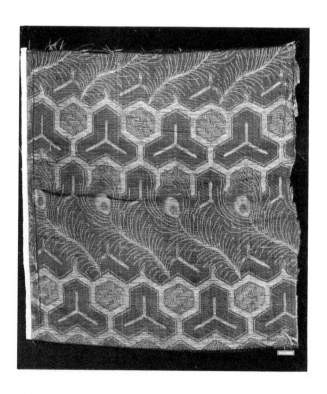

THE JAPANESE DESIGNER. Left: SILK BROCADE. Japan. 18th century. (The Victoria & Albert Museum, London.) Facing page: FOUR KIMONO PATTERNS. Photostats of drawings in a 2″ x 4″ rice-paper booklet of "patterns to be selected by printmakers or blockcutters to put on kimonos," according to O. Wang of the Mi Chou gallery, New York City, who owns the volume. These, and the examples on the two following pages, breathe pattern design at its purest. Where would you find more ingenious arabesque, or such brilliant combinations of two types of motifs? The designers of no other nation so easily run the gamut from peacock feathers to plaids.

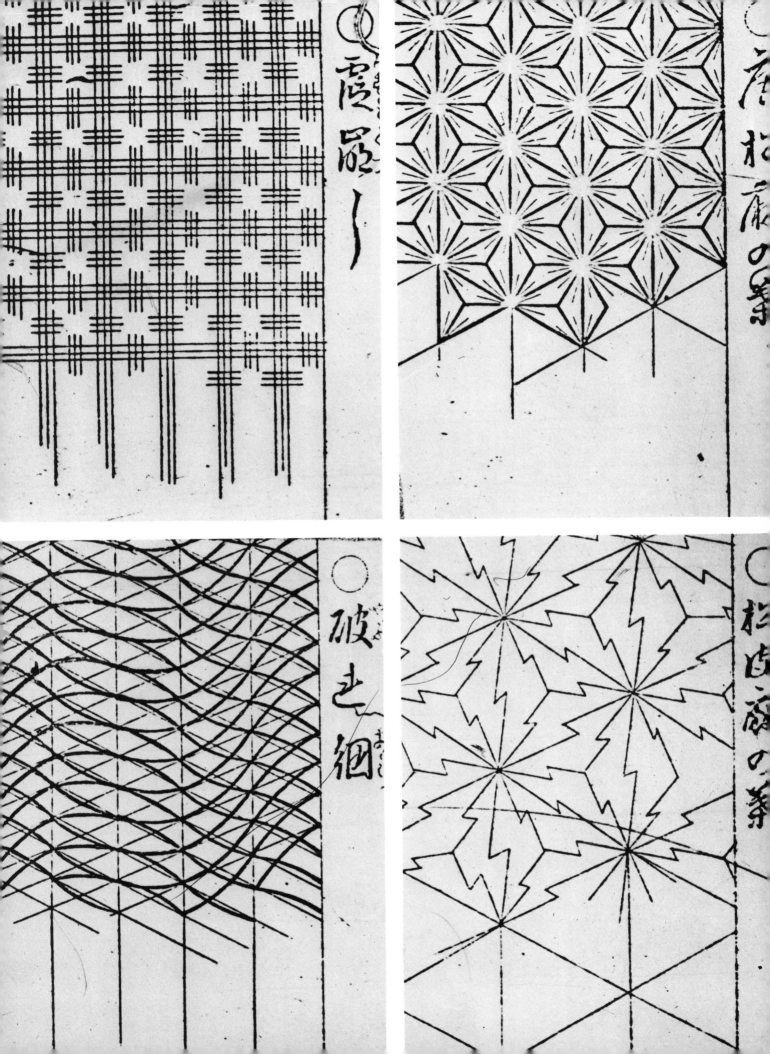

phoenix, with other mythical birds and beasts inhabiting thickets of peony-rosettes, appears unexpectedly in tapestries woven for Europe in colonial Peru. These are now a matter of record, and henceforth—after the eighteenth century—nearly everything is, or soon will be, a matter of record. As long as the knowledge in certain spheres was incomplete, and scholars, by their caution, showed they were guessing, there was no reason

TWO KIMONOS. Above: Kɪᴍᴏɴᴏ in the collection of Mr. Shinzo Noguchi, Tokyo. Facing page: Kɪᴍᴏɴᴏ in the Nagao Museum, Kamakura City, Kangawa. Both are pictured in Volume I of *Textile Designs of Japan* published by the Japan Textile Color Design Center, Osaka.

to refrain from making interpretations of my own, based on what any designer might observe. Beginning with the nineteenth century, however, there is no occasion for guesswork. Besides, all manner of pattern making has been indicated, if not explored. Toiles de Jouy, for example, are compositionally related to Persian figure-and-landscape patterns; Napoleon's Empire style owes quite as much to Imperial Rome as it does to his Egyptian campaigns. Following the Rococo period (itself an amalgam) all styles are virtually "revivals."

If we make an exception of William Morris in the last century, Art Nouveau at the turn of the century, and the Bauhaus in the twenties of this century, we find little that adds to our storehouse or our appreciation of pattern. Even these, viewed historically, seem slightly inconsequential. Morris had a genius for pattern, but it undeniably suffered from the taste of his times, and from his many other interests. Art Nouveau might be said to have extended Morris's "line of growth" to the point of strangling

itself. As for the Bauhaus, it instigated a method of art-inquiry which produced an impressive school of architecture and of advertising design, but nothing in the way of repeating surface decoration that begins to compare with patterns primitive people make the world over. In any case, we are much too close to these several styles, and to those of a few individual designers who have, more recently, achieved a style of their own. May history smile on them.

THREE FANTASIES. Facing page: STAIR HALL IN THE TASSEL HOUSE, BRUSSELS. 1892-93. Victor Horta. Art Nouveau. (Photograph courtesy The Museum of Modern Art, New York.) Above: Detail of EMBROIDERED BEDCOVER or HANGING. India-Portugal. (Courtesy, Museum of Fine Arts, Boston.) Overleaf: Sketch of a MOTIF ON A CHASUBLE OF FIGURED SILK. France. 17th century. Described as of Chinese inspiration, worked in silver and variegated colored silks on a satin ground, this bit of chinoiserie—evidently made from a fashionable dress into a vestment—ends our historical survey quite appropriately. Because, along with the deeper satisfactions we get from pattern, one of the most sought-after qualities is caprice.

The exercises that follow have, in themselves, no historical connections. To my knowledge, they have no educational precedent, either. As opposed to methods of pattern design that are based on geometry, or on nature, they proceed from the elements of design itself, gradually bringing these together in a way that design manuals—often working with the same elements—do not attempt to do. This could be called a grass-roots approach, and it seems to me just what pattern, at present, requires. Devised especially to train the eyes and hands of the novice pattern-maker, my method may also be of use to the professional who is interested in making new patterns rather than in remaking old ones. I hope so. We have been living on our pattern "capital" for a long time.

2

pattern making

eight lessons

THE POWER OF LINE ALONE. Pharoah's Army Submerged in the Red Sea. Woodcut. Italian. 16th century. Domenico dalla Greche after Titian. (The Metropolitan Museum of Art, New York. Rogers Fund. 1922.) Above: Detail of one of the twelve sections. Facing page: The entire composition. 5x7 feet. For many years I only knew the above section, and thought it complete and a masterpiece. To me it still tells the whole story.

line

Lesson 1

Original pattern design is not for everyone. It requires patience and determination; a willingness to do one thing at a time and to do it thoroughly. We cannot expect to improvise a good pattern any more than we can expect to improvise a sonata. Consequently, before we begin actual pattern-making, we must get acquainted with the different elements of design we will be using. These are four in number; namely, Line, Shape, Texture, and Color—not necessarily in the order of their importance, or of their appeal, which varies widely, but in the order we can most easily isolate them prior to putting them together. As I say, it is best to learn one thing at a time.

To design creatively it is imperative to see what we are doing from every viewpoint, without a chance of self-deception. Many pattern designers do most of their work at drawing boards, a habit I find incomprehensible. Even working in a hotel room I manage to have a 4- by 8-foot sheet of soft-pressed fiber (sold under various trade names, such as *Cellotex*) put in an adequate light against the wall. These panels take pushpins well, and not only give me a large working area but the opportunity, in fact the obligation, to study my work at all hours. A table for paints and brushes stands at one side, and when I am in a studio of my own there may be seven or eight of these panels around the room, sometimes butted together, each of them covered with reference material or patterns in progress.

But whether your easel surrounds you, as mine does, or is a card table or the side of a garage, patterning—of all sorts—begins with the drawing of guide lines. Do I hear sounds of lamentation? It seems one cannot mention the word "drawing" without loud wails from those who "can't draw a straight line," to which the answer is "Who said you had to?" Straight lines can be made with rulers, all lines can be made with mechanical aids, and in any case *to draw or not to draw* is really not much of a question.

Good patterns sometimes require verisimilitude, never a "likeness." If anything, it is a distinct advantage for a novice pattern maker to be an unskilled draftsman. Brilliant draftsmanship is fine for illustrators; for designers it leads to continual temptation—realism, fussiness, pretention. Consider how Henri Matisse, one of the great drawing masters of all time, stubbornly persisted in dissembling his skill. "Child-like?" Hardly. Deviousness in choosing a line is as characteristic of modern art as dissonance is of modern music.

Still, a modicum of manual dexterity is needed, even to make tracings. To overcome self-consciousness in drawing—which is largely due to what could be called papyruphobia, or fear of white paper—I suggest drawing on newsprint with sticks of charcoal, thick ones. Begin collecting selected pages of newspaper advertising immediately. A well laid out page of classified ads is an excellent example of Line patterning, while a full-page display ad set entirely in type is something to cherish. Start your exercises, however, on the less choice pages. Charcoal in hand, and preferably standing at an upright drawing board, begin by just making lines: firm, more or less straight lines at first, but evenly spaced; then curved, undulating lines kept equally distant from each other. As you continue, invent your own combinations of lines for these exercises. They can, if you wish, become quite poetic. Concentric circles of lines might expand like ripples in a pool. Or a series of lines might radiate from an unseen center to form circles suggesting seed dandelions. (The thinner sticks of charcoal in the box would be better, here.)

The idea of these first exercises is to begin to coordinate the hand and the eye, which is all that drawing actually amounts to. Jean Abel, my design teacher in high school, had her pupils use Chinese brushes and ink for practice purposes, but I think, now, that pointed brushes tend to give an overly-oriental look to a line. Today I would say that our most typical, vigorous line-makers are the felt-tipped marking pens which come in several widths, the ink drying instantly. A designer with good control of these pens has gone a long way towards achieving his own decorative signature.

Not that we should be too concerned about the *quality* of our lines at present. Remember "Original etchings, in limited editions, signed by the artist"? There are forms of preciousness, occasionally a fetish with graphic artists, which should be mistrusted by serious pattern designers. Hand-made-ness is high on the list. *Patterns ought to be equally effective whether produced by hand or by machine, by the yard or by the mile.* Wherever possible, a generous allowance should also be made for normal slip-ups in production. If your design idea depends critically upon *how* it is rendered, *how* it is printed, forget about it. Painstaking transcriptions of old techniques—steel engraving, wood block, batik—may be admirable in reproducing documentary designs, but in applying them to new patterns one runs the risk of parody and a cheap appearance. Furthermore, the technical problems can be appalling, as you will see later on. Surely it is worth while to collect and study examples of every kind of Line that

A MODERN MASTER. Facing page: THREE SHRIMPS. Ca. 1950. Ink on paper. Chinese. Chi Pai-shih. 1864-1957. (Photograph courtesy the Mi Chou gallery, New York.)

can be made, *provided* one recognizes the limitations of each one, and that each one is the result of using a certain kind of instrument on a certain kind of surface. Don't try to scrupulously imitate any of the examples you collect. They have nothing but inspiration to offer.

The highlights of a Line Collection might be as follows: Egyptian and other hieroglyphic and cuneiform styles, because of their economy and evocative power. Near and Far Eastern calligraphy for the opposite reason; who cares what, if anything, such elegant flourishes mean? Prehistoric pictures and primitive designs from all over the world—the various caves, and Oceania—which show such amazing observation and/or sense of decoration. Medieval and Renaissance sketches and prints of a once-scientific nature. Baroque architectural drawings for court spectacles. Drawings by Rembrandt, Hokusai, and Van Gogh, as I saw them "compared" in an exhibition at the Stedlijk Museum, Amsterdam, in 1951. This juxtapositioning struck me as a marvelous mode of revelation; one that could be used frequently: Paul Klee and Saul Steinberg; Tiepolo and Tchelitcheff. The neo-calligraphers belong somewhere, hereabouts, but how to disentangle them sensibly? One solution might be to select from Tobey, Pollock, Kline, Soulages, and Mathieu typical works that could not possibly belong to the others, and then pick out works of each which any one of them might have done. This could be still more instructive—to see what qualities modern arabesques have in common. A sampling of Spencerian, italic, and other types of penmanship and script would round out the collection nicely.

Line, in sum, is one of our most individual yet widely shared forms of expression, as witness our handwriting. For the last exercise of this initial lesson I suggest the most personal project imaginable: a real field day for the ego. Take a large sheet of paper—perhaps black kindergarden paper,

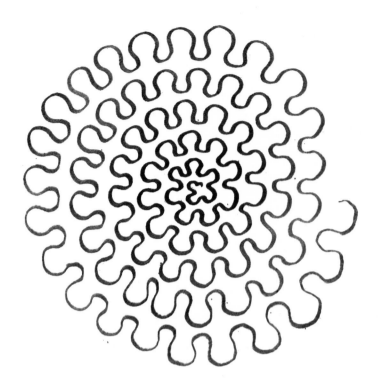

and a piece of white chalk—and write your name over and over, in many different sizes, until the sheet is completely filled. Is the result varied and interesting? Would it be improved by straighter lines, by grouping the lines, or if, here and there, you had indulged in a big Capital, or written at other angles? Perhaps the trouble is that your signature, itself, is chaotic: a scrawl in which you have come to take pride since that was easier than taking pains. So be it. A page of such graffiti, from time to time, will both clarify your hand and sharpen your sense of how to cover a given surface pleasantly, using words that are close to you. Style begins at home.

Summary

The four elements of design—LINE, SHAPE, TEXTURE, and COLOR—yield the best results when they are first explored separately. To avoid the discouragement of facing blank white paper, collect sheets of classified newspaper advertising. *Our first exercise is to make charcoal lines, of all kinds, on these sheets of newsprint.* Continue with this LINE exercise until the eyes and the hand are working together, and there is a feeling of control over the character and the spacing of the lines being drawn. When the results are pleasing, go over the lines with a felt-tipped marking pen. Meantime begin a LINE COLLECTION. Keep this in a folder for easy reference. *Our second exercise is a large page of calligraphy using your own name in its various forms. The idea is to cover a surface in a fluid, decorative manner rather than to make a series of static monograms.* Every time we write our name carefully we practice drawing.

EXERCISES IN LINE. Above and facing page: THE MARKING PEN. As one gains manual control through such exercises as those on the facing page, continuous-line drawings like the "petalled spiral" above should be attempted. This spiral would be effective on the inside of a bowl. Original drawing is 16 inches wide.

GLADYS BLAKE GLADYS BLAKE GLADYS BLAKE GLADYS BLAKE GLADYS
DYS BLAKE GLADYS BLAKE GLADYS BLAKE GLADYS BLAKE GLADYS BLAKE G
DYS BLAKE GLADYS BLAKE GLADYS BLAKE GLADYS BLAKE GLADYS BLAKE GLA
DYS BLAKE GLADYS BLAKE GLADYS BLAKE GLADYS BLAKE GLADYS BLAK
DYS BLAKE GLADYS BLAKE GLADYS BLAKE GLADYS BLAKE GLADYS BL
DYS BLAKE GLADYS BLAKE GLA DYS BLAKE GLADYS GLADYS BLAKE
DYS BLAKE GLADYS BLAKE GLA DYS BLAKE GLADYS GLA DYS BLAKE GLADYS

WHAT'S IN A SIGNATURE? Above: A Name Page by the author's pupil Gladys Blakeman. Facing page: Detail of Man With Violin. Pablo Picasso. 1910. (The Philadelphia Museum of Art. Louise and Walter C. Arensberg Collection.) A controlled signature, while no guarantee that it will become as valuable as Picasso's, is a sign that, with practice, one can draw whatever one wishes.

Lesson 2

For the first part of our second lesson we want to forget about "drawing" altogether. In spite of the signal success with Line of modern artists like Picasso and Matisse, Klee and Miro, line of itself is not an especially contemporary expression. The Middle Ages and the Renaissance used line just as persuasively, often in conjunction with the new printing methods that were being developed. But one form of Line long preceded the graphic arts and still seems able to surprise us. I refer of course to Stripes. They appear as painted decoration in the earliest Egyptian tombs (being at their most entrancing when they represent water as on page 32) and as an integral part of weaving nearly everywhere that textiles are found. It might be noted, in passing, that a pattern device as ancient and as universal as striping almost requires execution in what I call a "stubborn" medium. Otherwise it can look tawdry, provisional. But the stripes on the facades of Italian churches, or across the pavements of Brazilian beaches are both stimulating and satisfying largely because they are made of stone. That is, separate pieces had to be fitted together with energy and diligence—as though the material was resisting the process at every moment.

Do all stripes of distinction require a similar effort? It would appear that they do. I spoke of their ability to surprise us, thinking of certain Op Art experiments and the "magic moires" of Gerald Oster. Although these are a special breed of stripes, and sometimes extremely irritating, they do point up the importance of visual excitement, at least for the present time. On my first visit to New York, in 1936, I met a young woman who said she did "neckwear stripes," at a dollar and a half for each combination accepted. But no, she didn't know what made one banding more desirable than another unless, as she put it, it was because it had "class."

Undoubtedly many factors enter into our selection of stripes and I have often wondered, through the years, if our preferences could be classified according to national tastes. My findings, thus far, remain scanty and contradictory. Aside from a handful of unmistakable types like the "Roman" stripe, which is a matter of color, and the shaded "wave" stripe at the hem of Chinese ceremonial robes, which in reality is no more than a deep border, any of the familiar stripes can appear almost anywhere. At first glance a difference in degrees of civilization looked promising: stripes woven for Versailles as opposed to stripes woven in Arabia *Deserta*. Then, as my collection grew, it was also evident that social distinctions were meaningless. Civilized countries are apt to use the same dull mechanical striping over and over, while native weavers in a small backward country like Guatemala have distinctive stripes for each village and are always inventing variations. Could this imply that it is a mark of civilization, of fastidiousness, to accept the existing stereotypes? Woven in silk, naturally.

Let us see how many pleasing stripes we can produce in an hour or two. This is our chance, as I said, to avoid drawing; indeed, drawing would be

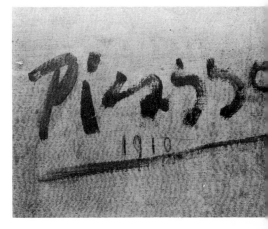

99

a waste of time. *The quickest way to visualize many effects is by means of overlays.* For stripes there is no better, quicker method. At this point someone is bound to suggest using tape, but it is less practical than it sounds, being hard to shift and hard to find in a good range of widths and tone values. Most art-supply stores stock so-called "construction paper,"

PART OF A LINE COLLECTION. Pictures chosen from a file of hundreds, for many reasons, including variety and individual curiosity-value. Above: BOWL. Glazed earthenware. Iran. 10th century. (Museum of Art, The Rhode Island School of Design.) Facing page: MARSHALL ISLANDS CHART. Obtained by Robert Louis Stevenson in 1890. Wave swells and their impact; the islands were once marked by tiny shells. (The University Museum, University of Pennsylvania, Philadelphia.) Overleaf: *MONTAGE.* Reading clockwise from top center: NEWSPAPER DISPLAY AD. (Reproduced with permission of Barton's Candy Corporation.) / HEAD. Colored pencil on black paper. Pavel Tchelitchew. 1950. (Collection, The Museum of Modern Art, New York.) / WE CARRY THE SUN TO THE STARS. Detail of large lace construction. Luba Krejci. Czechoslovakia. (Courtesy of the artist.) / TAPA CLOTH. New Guinea. (Collection of Max Ernst.) / WATCH THE BIRDIE. Magazine clip. (Courtesy Zeis Ikon-Voightlander, Inc.) / PEN FLOURISHING. (From *Pen Flourishing* by H. S. Blanshard. Courtesy of the publisher: Zaner-Bloser Co., Hand Writing Specialists, Columbus, Ohio.) / CHILD'S DRAWING. Traced from an adobe wall in Guatemala. / SHORE LEAVE. Detail of a wallpaper using tattoo designs drawn by Professor M. Zeis. / ELECTRONIC PATHWAYS. (Reprinted by permission of the Western Electric Company.) / ROOT MAN. Magazine clip. / PIER AND OCEAN. Charcoal, brush, and ink, heightened with white wash. Piet Mondrian. 1914. (Collection, The Museum of Modern Art, New York. Mrs. Simon Guggenheim Fund.) / WROUGHT-IRON GATE. Willi Tscherneck. Munich. / Other examples of Line are on pages 23, 33, 55, 194, and 212.

COLLECTION, THE MUSEUM OF MODERN ART, NEW YORK.

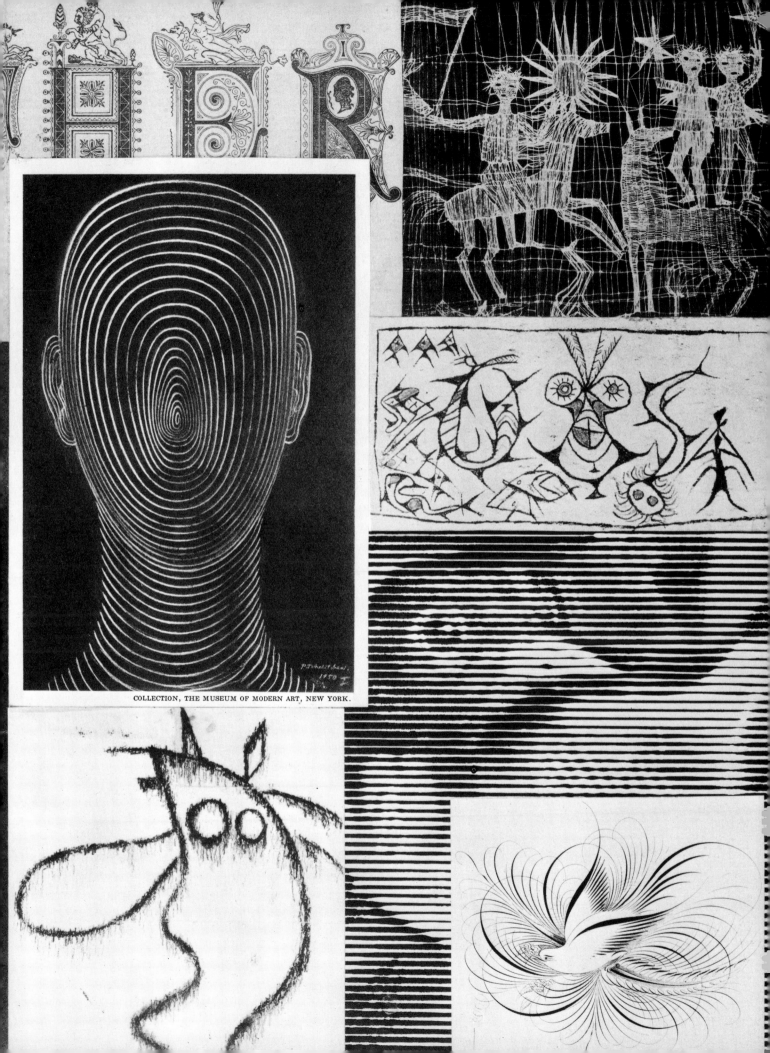

COLLECTION, THE MUSEUM OF MODERN ART, NEW YORK.

which comes in fairly large sheets and a number of strong colors. Since we are eschewing color for the time being, buy some of the white, the black, and the medium grey. Cut up a sheet of each into strips ranging from half an inch to several inches wide. Select a black or grey background and shift your contrasting bands of paper around on it until you have a stripe sequence—repeated at least once—that satisfies you. When you do, paste the strips down with rubber cement (which won't discolor the paper) and try for another stripe. There may not be much money in stripes but when you need them you need them badly.

Stripes, as you have gathered, have a physical presence of their own. However they are used, they command attention, so it is wise to learn their peculiarities. I don't mean that horizontals suggest repose, verticals suggest aspiration, and diagonals indicate danger; they do all these things, but to better advantage, in architecture and on sign-boards. What interests us, as pattern makers, is that stripes are quite literally a flag-waving device. Played down, in the backgrounds of historical fabrics, they assert their dignity; played up, in narrow, equal, strongly-contrasted lines they make the eyes jump, the surface pulsate. I am always entertained when Picasso uses stripes; they tell us the old showman is showing off.

And now to return to what is materially an extension of our own handwriting, exposed rather painfully in the previous lesson. *Sooner or later every artist develops a personal shorthand; the decorative artist in particular could not exist without a linear vocabulary at his fingertips.* The most comprehensive of these that I know of was worked out by the painter-designer Adolfo Best-Maugard. What he did was to analyze Mexican folk art and give it back to the modern Mexican craftsmen—and to us—as a system of all-purpose decoration. A similar job could be done on the popular art of Scandinavia, the Balkans, and India, to name a few places where an extensive design-language has been developed. The drawback to such systems is not their regional flavor (although this can be strong) but the invitation to endless proliferation that they offer. Edited and restrained, decorative "stenography" can be very useful.

There is, nonetheless, no substitute for the fresh observation of nature. This holds true regardless of the degree of abstraction desired. Picasso has said repeatedly that none of his work was abstract, by which he means, I take it, that he always has something specific in mind. This something is apt to be an existing style, e.g., the "classical" drawing of Ingres, or the hatched brushstrokes of Van Gogh, if not a particular painting such as Velasquez's "Maids of Honor." Pattern makers operate in much the same way. Each design falls into a category from which it derives its general mode, scale, and technique; then the details are supplied from patterns already on the market. More enterprising designers, on the other hand, have accumulated their own files of pictures which they augment with material borrowed from the Picture Collection of the local public library. Without fail, all of them have a few seed catalogues tucked away in a drawer. When I first came to New York, from California, I had the impression that New York designers never allowed themselves to look at fresh flowers!

But flowers, fresh, artificial, or pictured (baroque Dutch still-lifes are a prime source), have to be reckoned with; they constitute at least two-thirds of all our patterns. Let us call the next project Floral Shorthand, although we can only make a beginning. To get on the right track at once,

the paintings of Raoul Dufy will reward close study. Here are the bold abbreviations we want to emulate; Dufy doubtless arrived at some of them during the years he, too, designed patterns. Our own efforts to build up an alphabet, a repertoire of telling brushstrokes, couldn't be simpler. Take some ferns and grasses, artificial or real, and make a bouquet of them. Then lay in guide-lines with charcoal—and don't be afraid to smudge over lines you dislike; mistakes of this sort sometimes produce bright ideas. Take your brush or marking-pen in hand when you have what you want. Don't draw the container. *I usually compose such an arrangement on a piece of paper on the floor at my feet, looking down on it as if it were being seen against the sky.* Confine yourself to a black-and-white rendering using lines alone: dots and dashes, arcs, zigzags, cross-hatching. We are still learning to do one thing at a time.

Summary

LINES—in their most arresting form—are STRIPES. But effective stripes are less easy than they appear to be. They follow a plan, yet remain

STRIPES. Above: Actor's Mask. Oil. Paul Klee. 1924. (The Museum of Modern Art, New York. Sidney Janis Collection.)

105

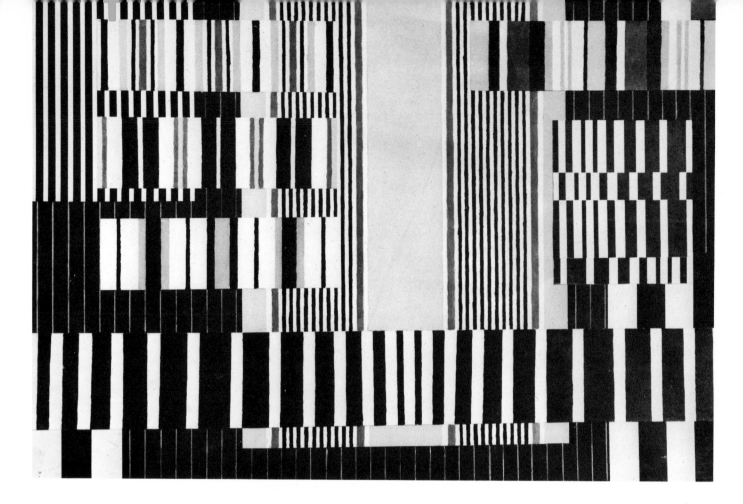

MORE STRIPES. Author's Collage. The mere names given to stripings are provocative: "chalk," "pin," "candy," "awning," "accordion," "prison," "ombre," and "Roman" stripe.

elusive. *In the first exercise of this lesson we shift around strips of construction paper of different widths and of several light-and-dark values, in order to visualize our ideas for stripes more quickly.* The best of these "instant stripes" should be pasted down and kept on file. Then we return to freehand drawing. *For our second exercise we arrange field flowers, grasses, or weeds in small bouquets, drawing them as simply as possible.* By repeating this exercise from time to time we gradually build up a system of graphic shorthand. Every pattern designer requires his own "language of flowers."

THE FLOWER PAINTING. Facing page top: Vase of Flowers. Jan Davidz de Heem. Dutch School. 1606-ca.1683/84. (The National Gallery of Art, Washington, D. C. Andrew W. Mellon gift, 1961.) Bottom: Still Life With Marigolds. Gouache. Raoul Dufy. Ca. 1934 (Photograph courtesy of the Charles E. Slakin Galleries, New York.) Floral subjects, as a rule, perfectly represent their period. In the Dutch painting, a window is realistically reflected in the glass vase. Dufy's Post-Impressionist manner not only expressed his time but it also gave the designers of the thirties and forties a new, highly-prized calligraphic technique.

A BOUQUET OF LINES. Overleaf: Weeds and Ferns. Chalk and charcoal on wrapping paper. By the author. This exercise is meant to "get something going" by arranging material that can be translated into simple strokes and still have style and the suggestion of movement. I couldn't resist the peacock feather.

shape

Lesson 1

During the foregoing exercises did you experience some difficulty in keeping your lines separate and distinct? It would be natural if you did, and all the more reason to get your hand under control. If lines merge or branch out they should do so by intention. The ultimate character of a pattern depends on each part of it being clearly defined; only then can the parts add up to an articulate and coherent whole. Our drawing lessons continue, now, with one important difference. Instead of keeping our lines apart, and terminating them before they lose their identity, we now turn them back upon themselves, making outlines—rather than lines —out of them. When these outlines are filled in, and are seen as silhouettes, the second element of pattern design, namely Shape, emerges.

We encounter outline and silhouette so frequently in the visual arts that we are seldom aware of them. Their potential as Shape goes unnoticed until a subject has been "stylized." Then we recognize them all at once—outline, silhouette, shape—because of their new, effective simplicity. Stylization means no more than that; it is the unity that results from kindred contours. For our Shape Collection, the best historical examples will differ considerably in scale. On the small side we will have medieval

ARPISM. Above: CONSTELLATION. Painted wood relief. Jean Arp. 1932. (The Philadelphia Museum of Art. Collection of Louise and Walter C. Arensberg.) Just as Picasso and Braque made us see the angularity around us, so Arp must be credited with isolating and making concrete the hitherto amorphous curved shape. Used with subtlety, as a fresh interpretation of the Baroque spirit, "Arpism" could be immensely useful to modern pattern designing.

責聯邦長期忽視
國內各城市問題
副總統促國會協助各市

一日起正式營業
六百餘中西生意

第四屆亞洲杯足球賽
中國隊一勝一和領先

許遠權病逝美京

劉宗賴逝世

越裁高樂向加拿大尋釁

象棋公開賽
中國觀眾已數百萬

太平痛飲變體酒
白傳醉吟彩鳳樓

題贈太白樓

紐約推行減鼠計劃撥巨款

昭倫公所秋祭

天氣報告

大埔投資公司
建第五頤養院

文化復興會成立

紐約州每年撥歉四百萬
向老鼠展開全面殲滅戰

美總統不滿軍費被評
未提及加稅籌軍文

illuminated picture-books and Eastern miniatures, simple in outline in order to be legible. On the large side we will have the frescos at the Villa of Mysteries, Pompeii, and those of Giotto and Fra Angelico farther north in Italy; these kept simple partly for technical reasons. Yet neither the older examples of silhouetted outline, such as these, or later specimens we have admired throughout oriental art and in Cubism, really prepared us for the impact of Shape as Hans (later Jean) Arp revealed it, sometime in the twenties.

The early "free forms" of Jean Arp seem like toys, today: a few turns of a jigsaw, mounted and painted white. Their power lay in their apartness. Other artists were using similar shapes, but in more elaborate contexts and with some reference to reality. Arp alone seemed to look at clouds and stones and parts of the human body with the sole idea of disavowing any connection with them. His own curved shapes, therefore, superficially natural-seeming as they are, stand firmly outside of nature. From there they *comment* on nature, as it were, and show other artists how to give all shapes a validity of their own. This procedure has been of inestimable value to men like Calder, Miro, Henry Moore, and, in his late years, Henri Matisse, although their success with it has been uneven. Sometimes they use free-form shapes expressively, sometimes not. Is this the same kind of "deviousness" we found was characteristic of the modern artist's approach to Line? Perhaps it is, and here the result can be most unfortunate. Whereas too much license with line merely gives an impression of incompetence, license with free forms gives us hideously amorphous furniture, wall "decor," and swimming pools. In the forties the landscape architect Thomas Church would throw a garden hose on the ground to get smoothly flowing outlines for his pathways and flower beds. But he questioned each curve. All of them had to be under exactly the right tension, to look logical and as if they belonged to their setting.

For the freedom of free-form shapes is qualified, like everything else. While they are not as strictly codified as Hogarth's "curve of beauty" or Art Nouveau's "whiplash" line, the contours of free form are faithful to their own curious unnaturally-natural figurations. One finds them in certain coral formations, in fungi, and in Chinese ginger roots. Our next exercise uses the last named, but if you can't buy them in a local Chinatown you can use root vegetables such as sweet potatoes, or use gourds, grapes, figs. Better still, draw enlargements of popcorn. Here, in a small, edible form, you have quasi-erotic shapes typical of twentieth century art. One warning, however. A little drawing, like a little learning, is a dangerous thing. Unless you select the above shapes with care and draw them with equal care, you won't learn much from them. Quality, in pattern making, depends on expressive shapes becoming related to other expressive shapes. By "expressive" I mean a shape produced under pressure. This condition is imperative. On the whole, shapes of our own look so contrived that I

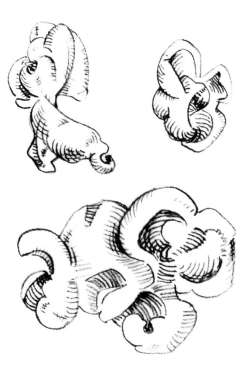

SUBJECTS THAT TEACH DRAWING. Facing page: GINGER ROOT and other Chinese vegetables. Felt pen on newsprint. Right: POPCORN. Pencil drawing.

PART OF A SHAPE COLLECTION. Above: CHASUBLE. Black silk crepe with white crepe appliqué. Henri Matisse. Ca. 1950. (Collection, The Museum of Modern Art, New York. Gift of Phillip C. Johnson.) Facing page: THE PAINTER'S WINDOW. Oil on canvas. Juan Gris. 1925. (The Baltimore Museum of Art. Bequest of Saidie A. May.) Gertrude Stein called Juan Gris "the perfect painter," and in this typical canvas the interlocking shapes make it clear that for pattern designers, too, he is the painter par excellence. Overleaf: *MONTAGE.* Reading clockwise from top center: PROPELLER SHOP. Magazine clip. / THE PINK NUDE. Oil on canvas Henri Matisse. 1935. (The Baltimore Museum of Art. The Cone Collection.) / Advertisement for MITSOUKO. (Courtesy of Guerlain's Perfumes, Inc.) / BIRD IN SPACE. Bronze. Constantin Brancusi. 1920-1924. (The Philadelphia Museum of Art. Collection of Louise and Walter Arensberg.) / The author's SHELL AND TABLE. Tempera. 1935. / INDIAN MINIATURE PAINTING. / SPANISH CAVALIER. Silhouette, paper. Hunt Diederich. (The Metropolitan Museum of Art. Gift of Edward C. Moore, Jr.) / Advertisement for SHALIMAR. (Courtesy Guerlain's Perfumes, Inc.) / CHERRIES. Photograph. Margrethe Mather. 1930. / Other examples of Shape are on pages 13, 22, 42, 189, and 222.

113

THE METROPOLITAN MUSEUM OF ART.

THE BALTIMORE MUSEUM OF ART.

Mitsouko by Guerlain

116

always prefer to adapt the curves or angles of natural objects (or the right piece of popcorn) for my major outlines. *By persevering in this exercise —and who except yourself will know whether you are getting a resemblance?—you will soon be able to draw anything and everything.*

Meantime a change of medium is indicated. As those who follow the course of modern art are aware, collages, or pasted papers, have influenced it profoundly. Painting has never been the same since Picasso stuck a bit of chair caning on an oval canvas in 1911. Thereafter, diverse printed matter appeared regularly on Cubist canvases; in Germany the small "merz" (as he called them) of Kurt Schwitters made liberal use of streetcar transfers. The illusion of reality created by this applied material was always negligible. Critics have described the early role of collage as "a reminder of the picture surface" and its flatness, while its fragmentary quality has obviously contributed to art's increasing decorativeness. This is the tendency I noted in the opening sentence of my Foreword when I said "Modern art is the celebration of design." And it is becoming that, more and more, in spite of the efforts of latter-day Dadaists and Surrealists to give their work psychological overtones by introducing incongruities. All this—from a bit of chair caning.

That there is a morbid aspect to Shape is undeniable. Rorschach blots always seem sinister to me; I suppose because they usually end in tentacles. The emotions that shape can summon are almost limitless. Victor Brauner, a shape specialist, is at once funny and disturbing. Alexander Calder achieves high drama with a few metal silhouettes in his larger stabiles; in the mobiles the mood is predominantly lyrical, notably in "The Forest is the Best Place" when the heavy "leaves" slowly turn and turn. Juan Gris is another artist whose works rely mostly on shape. A romantic Cubist, his best pictures are masterpieces of construction, puzzles one never tires of. A favorite device of Gris's is the common, or shared, outline: the side of a compote which is also the side of a pear; a glass of wine wedded to a pipe and a book. These are not Hard Edge paintings, as we know the genre today, but they do look as if their components could have been cut from stiff paper.

Our own scissor-work will be of two kinds. First we will follow shapes as they are, then we will alter them by using our imagination and what we have learned from the various artists whose mastery of shape is so striking. All we need is a small pair of sharp shears and a few sheets of construction paper. Taking a hint from Matisse's last period, we might begin by cutting out some tropical leaf-shapes (preferably not the over-used split-leaf philodendron). That is the crux of the matter: we need a model to refer to. Otherwise, relaxed and unchecked, our scissors will turn out nondescript shapes of no interest to anyone. To guard against this, select your material carefully. One day, needing money more than usually, I

SHAPES THAT CHANGE. Facing page top: SPIDER. Standing mobile. Painted sheet aluminum and steel wire. Alexander Calder. 1939. (Collection, The Museum of Modern Art, New York. Gift of the artist.) Bottom: DIALOGUE AVEC L'ANTI-MOI. Oil on canvas. Victor Brauner. 1963. (Photograph courtesy the Alexander Iolas Gallery, New York.) Calder's mobile shapes really do change as they shift, whereas Brauner's painted shapes change with the viewer's attention. Equivocal space has always played a role in pattern making and the current interest in optical illusions is rapidly extending the range of these phenomena. It will be a great day for the pattern designer when geometric illusions and Surrealist images merge.

went to the park, picked up a dozen different leaves, arranged them in a simple pattern, with attention to the spacing, and then sold it to the first firm I called on. That's one way to make Shape work for you.

Another way is by distortion. *Some shapes have become so hackneyed that to take liberties with them is to do them a kindness.* Butterflies, for instance. The glass cases at museums of natural history contain an occasional specimen of memorable shape; the majority, considered without color and markings, are strictly standard. Butterflies, like most flowers, need to be seen with fresh eyes. That's where distortion comes in, one of the oldest modes of art, now a cornerstone of modernity. But distortion without reference to reality lacks substance. Here our scissors can give yeomen service. For most of us they are a fairly awkward instrument. Give them their head, so to speak. Bearing in mind the species of shapes we are after, but cutting them out freehand and freely, new flora and fauna should fall from our scissors like manna from heaven.

Summary
When we continue a line and close it we create a SHAPE. Our SHAPE COLLECTION—which may include pictures of three-dimensional forms —will embrace all images that exhibit an eye-catching silhouette. Like each collection, it should be kept in a folder or put on file. *Our first exercise is again a drawing lesson. It involves making outline drawings of any shapes that are sufficiently unusual* not to require a "resemblance." The

purpose is to increase our appreciation of abstract SHAPE. Then, once more, we put aside our drawing materials and pick up our construction paper and a pair of scissors. *In the first of our two paper-cutting exercises we follow the outlines of house-plants as faithfully as possible.* Possibly we find that nature's shapes are not always fascinating. *In the second cutting exercise we allow ourselves freedom to interpret or distort nature so that it is fascinating.* All three exercises have the same ultimate purpose. A pattern is only as interesting as the shapes that go into it.

SOUVENIRS FROM THE PAST. Facing page: PRESSED LEAVES, 1945. Above: JEWELED BUTTERFLIES, 1953. Both are first sketches by the author for patterns made from material found in New York's Central Park and items seen in San Francisco's Chinatown, respectively. Some of the butterflies were semi-precious ornaments on a lacquer screen, others were hair ornaments. Right: MARBLE BUT-TERFLY. A paper cut-out sufficiently distorted to be of interest today.

Lesson 2

The part that Shape plays in pattern design can scarcely be exaggerated. Not only do shapes pervade a good pattern and substantiate its style, but in larger units they provide the structure. Line alone cannot do this; that is why I felt it was premature to discuss the actual making of a pattern until we had something more tangible to work with—to build with. Because a pattern is, in many respects, much like a building. It is made up of units, or shaped masses, and these masses must be put together in one, or a combination, of a certain limited number of ways; otherwise they won't work. That is to say they won't "repeat" and become a pattern.

With the possible exception of stripes, all all-over patterns can be reduced to two basic plans, the "block" and the "brick." (A polka dot is merely a spot *within* an invisible block or brick.) As you see in the diagram, the block repeat is a straight match—horizontally as well as vertically—whereas the brick repeat also matches straight across, from side to side, but is staggered, or overlapped, above and below. By turning the block repeat at a 45-degree angle we get the useful lozenge or "diamond"

THE DROPPED AND REVERSED MOTIF. Left: Sprig Pattern. Redrawn from a brocaded silk velvet with voided pile. Italy. Late 16th century. Facing page: The Harvesters. Block-printed cotton designed by Raoul Dufy. 1923. (The Cooper Union Museum. Au Panier Fleuri Fund, 1934.) Both patterns are constructed according to the same plan; in the Dufy it is ingeniously concealed.

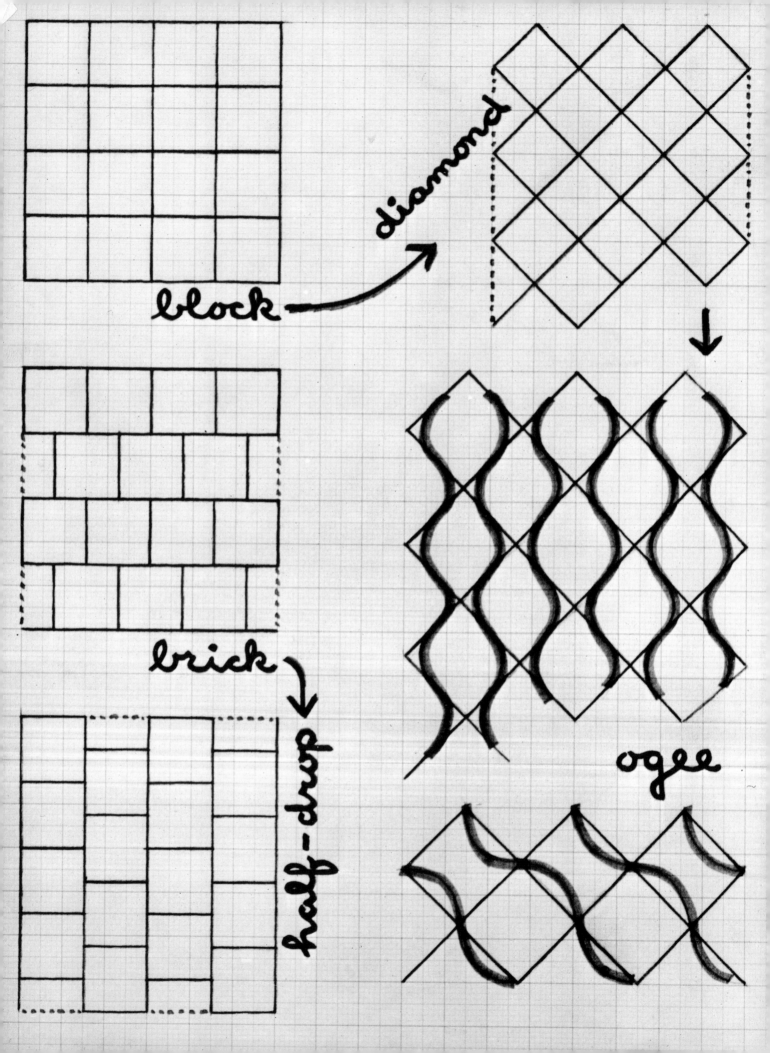

block → diamond

brick → half-drop

ogee

arrangement, while the equally useful "half-drop" layout is simply the brick repeat turned on its side. From this point on, new repeats lie mainly in the viewing. A fifth and sixth repeat make use of what is called an ogival or "ogee" framework. This is the result of undulating lines drawn to the left and right of diamonds placed in a vertical position or at the top and bottom of diamonds laid out horizontally, with both layouts subject to being tilted. But these schemes, you say, give the effect of a continuous stripe. They do. But what are stripes except a string of more or less contiguous blocks? The reason stripes seem to have repeating characteristics of their own is that their components can assume so many guises. In addition to being "broken," yet forming a line, stripes can be placed in a vertical, horizontal, or diagonal position, and, furthermore, be either angular or curving. Their independence, nonetheless, is largely an illusion. Upon scrutiny all stripings, however complicated, can be reduced to a block or a brick layout. And the same holds true of such secondary motifs as appear at the intersections of a framework, or in the all-over patterning of a background. Whatever their relative importance, all the parts of a pattern follow the same few ground rules. And once their relationships have been established—for, as I said, several types of repeat may be combined in one pattern—all parts will function as a single unit.

To protest this scheme of things is futile. If you try to put completed drawings together without spacing them on an appropriate (but usually invisible) framework your chances of avoiding "bull's eyes" and "rivers" are nil. Bull's eyes are undesirable focal points which leap out at you, at regular intervals; rivers are made up of accidental repetitions which form unexpected, unwanted bands. Both occur when pattern makers rebel—

A PAGE OF "REPEATS," AND A PATTERN THAT SHOWS HOW THEY WORK. Facing page: THE WAYS PATTERNS CAN BE PUT TOGETHER. Above: Author's rough sketch of PASSION FLOWERS, in casein, to suggest a semi-naturalistic floral stripe based on the ogival or "ogee" framework.

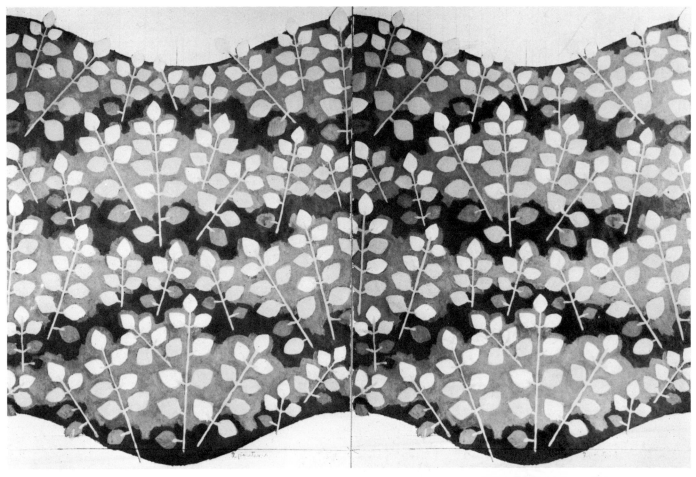

FOUR STAGES OF A SINGLE PATTERN. Facing page
top: The first sketch for TREETOP, a wallpaper or printed
fabric pattern. Casein on paper. Bottom: A second sketch
laid out in charcoal on architect's cross-section paper.
Above: A paste-up of two photostats made after the charcoal version had been painted in. In this version, made to
check the side match, it can be seen that the ogee stripe,
which has been used horizontally, forms too straight a line
in one place. This must be corrected, or the eye will pick
it up at once. Also, there should be less regularity in the
undulating lines, more variety in the leaves. Right: Detail
of final rendering ready for the screen-maker. All shapes
have become definite, but the slight "halo" around the
leaves will soften them by letting the ground show through.
Prepared for reproduction in four colors.

as they often do—against the strictures of their trade. This rebellion is usually related to the "studied carelessness" we practiced in the late thirties. Studied carelessness consists of scattering motifs around rather loosely, in the hope that their casual distribution will distract from the repeat's actual rigidity. To further the informal atmosphere a half-drop layout is frequently employed, for the eye does not readily pick out a unit unless identifying marks appear, as expected, side by side. Unhappily, all half-drop repeats need continual rechecking, since the inadvertent effects, noted above, have a bad habit of appearing out of nowhere. It is true that there are "repeating glasses" you can buy, which put a single unit in multiple repetition (including a drop effect, if you pay more), but I find the only certain way to avoid bull's eyes, rivers, and—what to me is worse —areas that are too crowded is to have four photostats made when a sketch is nearly finished. Then I can study, at leisure, every nuance of distribution, also checking the "match," at top, bottom, and sides.

At this point no drawing exercise would be as valuable as an analysis of the patterns you see around you. Are they put together as blocks? As bricks? Has a half-drop repeat been used? A diamond network? If the patterns on hand are too few or too obvious, get some remnants of printed drapery material in a department store basement and do a thorough autopsy on them. When you have found the unit of repeat, cut out several and try them in the other positions diagrammed above, either by pinning

SHAPE AS STRUCTURE. Facing page: Palm Trees. Author's printed drapery fabric for J. H. Thorpe—a perfect specimen of the "diamond" repeat. Above: Pattern based on the cartouche-shaped Flower Beds at Antigua, Guatemala, which are raised up just high enough to be tended without bending over.

the motifs to a plain piece of cloth or laying them out on the floor. An hour of this exercise should acquaint you with the merits of the various repeats as they pertain to different kinds of motifs. Now go through the drawings you have been making—whether for Line or Shape—and chose a few "motifs" of your own. While doing so, their possible arrangement in a pattern will suggest itself. Go along with these suggestions. Buy some cross-section paper such a architects use, and rough in, with charcoal, the positions your motifs are to occupy. From your samples of fabric, or perhaps of wallpaper, you can get a general idea of the width and height of repeat required, commercially, as accurate as any measurements I could give you. Each manufacturer wants slightly different dimensions depending on the mechanical methods he uses. All you need, now, is to visualize what will happen when a definite unit is repeated over and over. By committing your ideas to graph or cross-section paper you move into the realm of professional design.

Are some repeats better than others? In all the arts, it is considered ideal when form and content coincide. In pattern design, this means that the motif—the content—is such that it constitutes the repeat—the form. The perfect and alas all too prevalent example is the damask type of pattern in which motif and structure are inseparable. Here, since true damasks are a reversible weave and "read" just as well from either side, the balance between figure and ground cons the eye into accepting all damask patterns as being of a superior order, elegant and regal. On the contrary, most of those we see today are completely bastardized by years of hasty adaptation to varying mechanical requirements. Damask patterns have been around a long time, too long not to have suffered many alterations. Badly warmed-over late Renaissance motifs are the worst. The better damasks are Gothic or early Renaissance.

Fortunately there are other patterns, beside the dubious damasks, in which form and content, structure and subject matter are highly congenial. Some of these, too, are anachronisms, though they need not be. There is, for instance, the shape-enclosing-other-shapes which occurs in the popular form we call a "paisley" pattern. Yet this need not utilize leaf or "cone" shapes as it originally did in India. In Turkish versions,

carnations are tucked into tulips to make some of the most delectable designs in existence. What I am suggesting is that you think about shapes-within-shapes as a means of simultaneously building a pattern and embellishing it. How about Arks filled with animals? Too childish? How about human shapes—somewhat distorted—filled to an invisible outline with rough, many-pointed stars?

The cartouche is another strategem of ancient pattern-making which could be beneficially revived, especially since paisley patterns threaten to outdo damask in number and careless adaptation. Essentially the cartouche is a frame, although it is described as a "scroll" from its legend-bearing function on old maps; hence, I suppose, its name. I see the cartouche, however, not as a way of presenting an inscription but as a means of activating a whole surface with related shapes. These shapes, which would naturally provide the pattern's framework, might take their outlines from many sources: fretwork, marquetry, the sections of a sweetmeat box, the parterres of an elaborate garden. They would not necessarily be symmetrical around a central axis. Venetian mirrors, like twisted valentines, could provide the kind of divisions I have in mind.

We conclude our second lesson on shape by again looking to a painter. He is René Magritte, the Belgium surrealist, and he restores to Shape all the poetry Jean Arp once sought to ignore. We see, in Magritte's canvases, how closely shape approximates literature, as it does when a landscape "becomes" a nosegay in a window, vase and all, or a nosegay substitutes for a tree. Such transpositions—of one group of objects taking the place normally occupied by another so that the images become interchangeable—is entirely within the range of pattern making. So is a playful use of perspective, as in our illustration. Because of its affinity with toiles de Jouy, always a favorite with people who cannot resist quaint pictures, this slightly askew pictorialism is certain to be one of the directions pattern will explore when it becomes a creative art form again.

Summary

SHAPE gives us our first opportunity to make repeating patterns, a "repeat" being a shaped unit which combines with other units in accordance with one or more of the diagrams on page 122. *Using these diagrams as a guide, we analyze, take apart, and reassemble a number of existing patterns which have several different types of repeat.* Now we are ready to construct a pattern of our own, with some of the drawings we made earlier as our subject-matter. *On architect's cross-section paper we lay out a block, a brick, and a half-drop repeat big enough to accommodate rough tracings of the motifs selected.* It is now a question of learning by seeing and doing. For those who have some mastery of the repeat, less obviously geometrical frameworks are proposed. The Orient in particular uses SHAPE as a series of interlocking compartments, sometimes one inside of another, as in a Chinese puzzle.

NEAR AND FAR. Left: LA CASCADE. Oil on canvas. René Magritte. 1961. (Photograph courtesy of the Alexander Iolas Gallery, New York.) The illusion of depth is normally an enemy of good pattern design, but this is so because there is usually an intention to deceive. Magritte makes no pretense of illusion. A master of the "double-take," he practises his legerdemain openly, and we see, but find it hard to say, exactly what is happening.

texture

Lesson 1

Lines are seldom sharp and clear. Shapes are rarely smooth and solid-looking. We would not want them to be. In earlier days the problem took care of itself. Either the material on which a pattern was printed had a broken surface or the available printing techniques made it seem so. Well, those good, crude old days are gone forever. Replacing them, what do we find? Fake patinas, "distressed" surfaces; all the earmarks of art forgery. This is understandable enough in the manufacture of reproductions, but where does it belong among modern products? To apply the ravages of time to old and new styles alike is patently ridiculous.

Yet this is what happens during the processing of commercial patterns. As the incentive to create original designs diminishes, the effort to give a spurious interest to the existing stock-pile increases. My own introduction to artificial aging was a line of hand-blocked fabrics from Italy I saw in the thirties. I thought them attractive, but somehow fraudulent and unimportant. A resurgence of original patterns was occurring at the time and meretricious elegance didn't disturb me. What I failed to see then was that this kind of counterfeit quality could lead to an emphasis on Texture out of all proportion to the part it should play in creative design, and would eventually result in what is now known as "mucking up" or "the one-hundred per cent coverage treatment" so rampant today.

Texture has become cause for suspicion, a disguise for mediocrity. Therefore, the study of this, our third element of design, must be approached with caution. Delicate decisions are involved. In this plastic-coated, detergent-cleaned era, smooth-looking surfaces can be as practical as any others, but apparently the general public—according to manufacturers—is not aware of this. The public has been conditioned to expect texture, and texture it must have, real or simulated, appropriate or inappropriate. While we can dismiss, at once, the softening-up formulas, the mincing brushstrokes that the average commercial designer uses in rendering a finished sketch (see almost any wallpaper or drapery material) *we must still find ways to avoid insistently hard, sharp edges when printing on anything but an actually uneven surface.*

In some cases the subject itself will suggest how it can be rendered. As you gather pictures for your Texture Collection you will notice that everything in nature has markings. Flowers have veins, branches have ridges, birds are feathered, and most animals are hairy. Man-made objects also show surface variations. New objects are regular and sometimes reflective, old ones are marred and sometimes encrusted. These are the clues

THE BROKEN SURFACE. Snow Storm: Steamboat Off a Harbour's Mouth. Oil on canvas. J. M. W. Turner. 1842. (The National Gallery, London.) Turner was 66 years old when he painted this, and is said to have had himself lashed, like Ulysses, to a ship mast in order to observe the storm.

PART OF A TEXTURE COLLECTION. Above: Bird Singing in the Moon-
light. Gouache. Morris Graves. 1938-39. (Collection, The Museum of Modern Art,
New York.) Facing page: Ecco. Plastic, wood, shell, bone, glass, mirror, and metal
embedded in plastic, on honeycomb board. Alfonso Ossorio. 1963-66. (Photograph
courtesy of Cordier & Ekstrom. New York.) While both the painting by Graves and
the panel by Ossorio have much interest beyond their broken surfaces—the poetry
of one, the jewel-like color of the other—it is also true that their varied textures add
to the visual experience, as they do in the pictures that follow. Overleaf: *MONTAGE*.
Reading clockwise from top center: Detail of Display Ad. (Reproduced with permission of Barton's Candy Corporation.) / Night Sky. Magazine clip. / Savanna.
Oil on canvas. Gonzalo Ariza. 1942. (Collection, The Museum of Modern Art, New
York. Inter-American Fund.) / The Cow with the Subtile Nose. Oil and duco on
canvas. Jean Dubuffet. 1954. (Collection, The Museum of Modern Art, New York.
Benjamin and David Sharps Fund.) / Detail of Display Ad. / Author's Tony with
a Sparkler. Casein. 1953. (Courtesy of Mr. and Mrs. Edward Cannon.) / Street
Light. Oil on canvas. Giocomo Balla. 1909. (Collection, The Museum of Modern
Art, New York. Hillman Periodicals Fund.) / Crab. Newspaper clip. / Springtime.
Gouache and pastel. Tancredi. 1952. (Collection, The Museum of Modern Art, New
York. Gift of Peggy Guggenheim.) Other examples of Texture are on pages 14, 16,
199, 210, and 221.

133

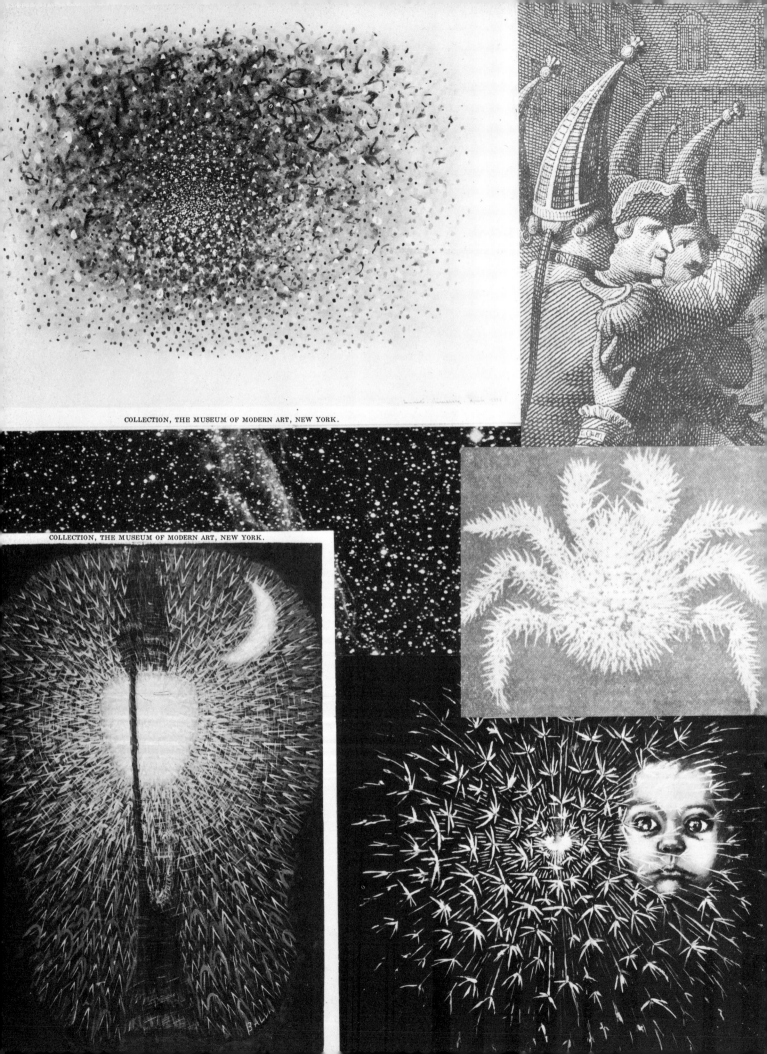

COLLECTION, THE MUSEUM OF MODERN ART, NEW YORK.

COLLECTION, THE MUSEUM OF MODERN ART, NEW YORK.

captions, lunch under the great tree. An
reflections of the sparkle and spirit of
and rare to see and remember. All at
There's nothing like it back home.

Marshall Field

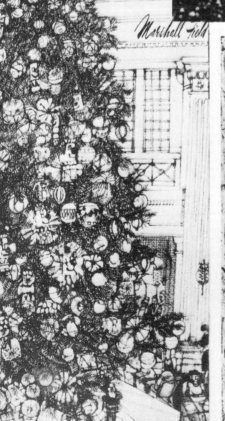

COLLECTION, THE MUSEUM OF MODERN ART, NEW YORK.

COLLECTION, THE MUSEUM OF MODERN ART, NEW YORK.

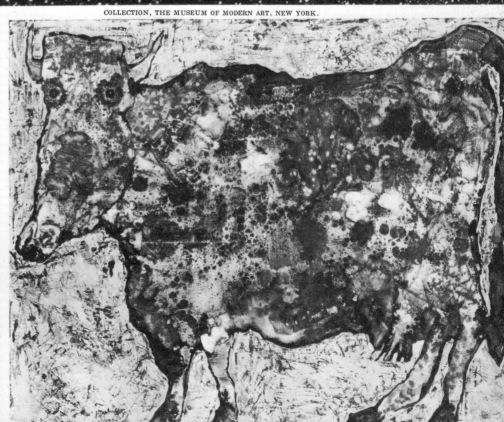

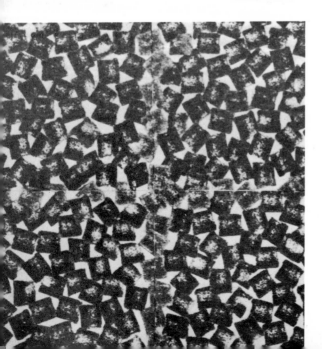

LOTS OF DOTS. Left: EXERCISE SHEET OF SPOTTINGS. Described on page 137. The middle exercise is quartered, to make a new center, then filled in, at bottom. Facing page: Detail of author's collage STAMP COLLECTION. At a short distance the individual stamps blend into a lively surface of pointillist color. Their identity is what gives the pattern its character, but at the present time it would have to be reproduced by rotogravure or the four-color process: expensive methods for a novelty.

to follow in quest of individual textures. A study of the surfaces of certain paintings would not be amiss, either. Although printed surfaces can only hint at heavy impasto, we are bound to gain freedom for our brushes by looking at masters as ostensibly different as Courbet and Albert Ryder, Rubens and André de Segonzac. What a range of qualities! Dignity, voluptuousness, violence, and, above all, mystery. For texture is unequalled in creating atmosphere. Totally unlike each other as they are in using Texture, where would Odilon Redon, Yves Tanguy, and Morris Graves be without it?

Our own investigation of texture begins with the simple dot, spot, or mark; a felt-tipped marking pen our modest implement. The aim is to achieve equal distribution; first, with a stippled surface similar to what you see in the strict Impressionism—or, more exactly, the *pointillisme*—of Seurat and Signac. This sounds easy, until you try it! After a few minutes you will find your coverage getting too thick, then too thin. It is naturally possible to fill in the empty spaces, but it is much better to keep starting over, on new sheets of paper (small tablet sheets are ample) until you develop a steady rhythm. While employing such "motor skills" I always listen to music, not so much from boredom as to keep from thinking. Pattern making is full of these mechanical periods when only the hand and eyes are involved.

After dots, let's try dashes. Dashes, in varied forms of cross-hatching, are the time-honored favorite of engravers and printmakers—not that we intend to emulate Piranesi or Gustave Doré. To be useful to us, this exercise, too, must aim at clear-cut, uniform coverage. At the end of the exercise some of our sheets should look as if they were covered with hundreds of tiny jackstraws. We could, of course, continue these exercises indefinitely, making textures out of all kinds of marks—checks, crosses, blots—with all manner of implements—old brushes, palette knives, sponges. But there is a danger that the results will be too striking: a handicap to a good pattern. The advantage of the two simplest textures—stippling and cross-hatching—is that they break up a surface unobtru-

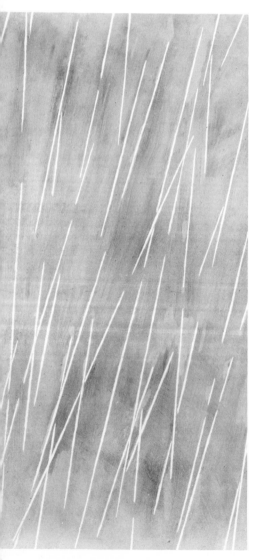

sively. Either of them can provide us with shaded areas, with backgrounds, or with a softening over-print. In the two latter cases, if the texture extends over the whole repeat, it will be necessary to get an exact "match," at top and sides, by quartering the paper and rearranging the sections according to the layout on page 136. This will bring the contiguous inner sides of the unit to the outside, where they will "join"—and to make a new center is a matter of minutes.

What we must shun, in working with texture, are lovely subtleties that cannot be produced, or once produced cannot be repeated. Student designers, seeing how prominently happy accidents figure in modern painting, feel that they too should cultivate them, not realizing that painting and the reproductive processes of printing are poles apart. Photography can bridge some of the gaps, but, as you will see in the next lesson, mechanical processes have a style of their own. So, to paraphrase what I said in connection with Line: if your design idea depends critically on the faithful imitation of a texture, forget about it. Rubbings and crackling, washes and scrumbling should be translated into firm impressions before they become part of a pattern. Then, obviously, they can be printed by whatever method is most suitable. I labor this point because Texture has an enormous fascination for the amateur. He sees it as a means of minimizing his mistakes and even of imbuing them with grandeur. This has led to a wide abuse of transparent colors and endless "experiments" with over-printing. The results look like what they are: improvisations in search of a pattern.

When you have gained control of stippling and cross-hatching, I suggest that you apply them, discreetly, to some of the patterns you have laid out. At first you could cut small overlays from your "exercise" sheets; this will give you an idea of whether the dots and/or dashes should be coarser in some places, finer in others. A variety in the denseness of these textures might also be rewarding, for it would, when printed, produce stronger color where the marks are close together. From these exercises in what is, substantially, a form of shading, it is only a step to the development of markings, such as broken lines, which can indicate direction, or depth, for your shapes. This is often desirable for defining the parts of a complex ornament, and is a natural accompaniment to rendering leaves and other growing things. Finally, you might consider Texture as something to be used throughout an entire pattern, giving it a semblance of having been woven, carved, embroidered, etcetera. But don't be too convincing! Easy does it.

Summary

A preoccupation with textured effects has discouraged original pattern design throughout the decorative arts industry. Yet TEXTURE has its legitimate uses, and the exercises for producing uniformly broken-up surfaces are a valuable discipline. *This lesson falls into two parts. First, the textures themselves and whether they will print as rendered. Second, the procedure for making a "match" as described above and illustrated on page 136—an exercise which may be necessary when textures are continuous at the edges of a repeat.* It is suggested, in passing, that nature and the fine arts should contribute equally to a Texture Collection, and finally it is noted that if TEXTURE is used with discretion and a light touch it can become an asset to a pattern rather than a disguise or a disaster.

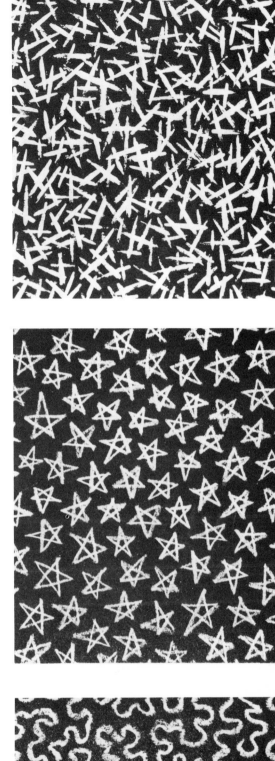

LOTS OF LINES. Facing page: Detail of the author's wallpaper pattern RAIN, ca. 1948, for Katzenbach and Warren, suggested by a Hiroshige print. Right: EXERCISE SHEET OF MARKINGS. The marks at the top are from a brush laid on its side, those in the middle use Jean Cocteau's star insignia, and at the bottom, we see the filler-motif called "vermiculation."

Lesson 2

Once again we dispense with freehand drawing. In a mechanized period
like ours it would be naïve to bypass technical tricks and processes which
have long been available to the printing industry and are now being exploited by Pop and Op Art, which—to a large degree—are extensions of
the comics and of advertising. The origin of their most characteristic
effect is the screen used for making halftone reproductions from photographs. Look at a book or newspaper halftone illustration through a mag-
nifying glass and you will see that, in reality, it is made up of tiny dots.
This translation of an image into small opaque particles is necessary in
order to print it. Fundamentally it is the same problem we encountered
in the last lesson, except that in halftone reproduction the texturing is
entirely mechanical and, to the naked eye, invisible.

It is Texture just the same. The craft of photo-engraving goes back
more than a hundred years, and I dare say its pioneers would be dismayed
at how thoroughly their efforts are being reversed. Men like Fox Talbot
strove to eliminate textures from graphic art just as doggedly as Roy
Lichtenstein strives to return it. I was first conscious of coarsely-screened
pictures in the top fashion magazines—where a new look is a constant concern—and now they have become routine in advertising. The gimmick,
although a obvious one, could nevertheless be useful in pattern making.
While the industry pays lip service to freshness, novelty, as such, is mis-

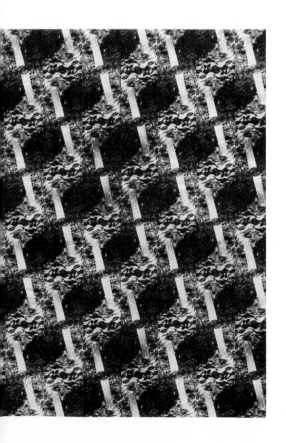

PATTERN BY PHOTOGRAPHY. Left: Post and
Shells. Multiple photographic print. Thurman Rotan.
1945. Facing page: Fan Stripe. Margrethe Mather and the
author. 1930. The camera does only part of the job. For the
Rotan print, a single picture was turned upside down to
obtain a "texture," which, as Mr. Rotan says, "might be
translated into weaving." In the Mather print we were
concerned to present "decorative images suitable for industry" in an exhibit at the De Young Museum, Golden Gate
Park, San Francisco. But most of our prints would have
required considerable retouching before they made
smoothly continuous patterns.

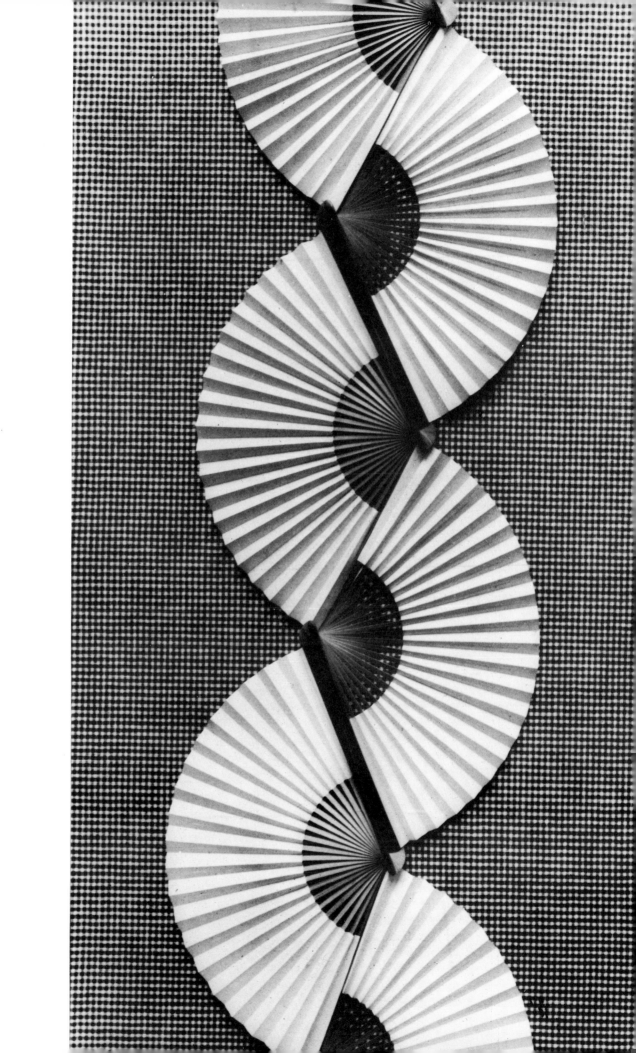

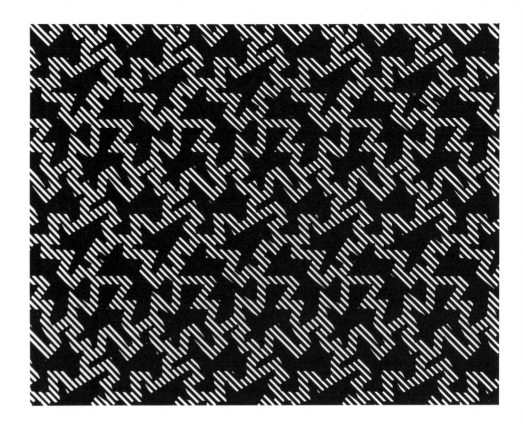

trusted; the pattern field is notoriously conservative. New techniques must be absorbed by familiar subject matter before they attain real currency.

Do you know a friendly photographer? If so, ask him to shoot one of your smaller, more solidly rendered patterns through a processing screen. Then, for study purposes, have a good-sized enlargement made from the negative. Of recent years an appalling amount of skill has been expended on applying simulated textures to sundry patterns, batik enjoying a special vogue. This is a sad and silly abuse of technical know-how, for an image broken down into a network of minute lines is, decoratively, quite worthless. "Shading screens," of so many dots per line in graded percentages of solidity, and what are called "pattern sheets," which are equivalent to the sheets of stippling and cross-hatching we made in the last lesson, should be used as the mechanical expressions they are. These highly conventionalized textures, arrived at through photography, would be a boon to many contemporary patterns whose chief claim to modernity is brashness. A stylized softening of the surface would help them.

Going still further along mechanized lines, how are we to use the findings of Op Art? The pattern potential here is staggering. Irony is added to the situation, because the Op artists of today consistently capitalize on the kind of effects that pattern makers have always sought to avoid.

TEXTURE BY PROCESS SCREEN. Above: Detail of author's pattern CRAZY KEY as it looks when printed through a striped screen. Facing page: The same pattern (which also appears on the dust-jacket) with marbelizing imposed. This trick, of both having your pattern and pulverizing it, is highly esteemed in commercial circles, but a better way to soften an image is to print it in close values.

144

To put optical illusions in repeat is easy enough, but are the resulting patterns really useful? Time and again, through the centuries, optical illusions have been a kind of scientific toy. When the novelty wears off, this time around, what will we have that we did not have in Roman pavements and the perspective fantasies of the fifteenth century?

To what extent pattern can benefit from science itself remains, at least for me, just as questionable. In the wake of Cubism everyone saw nature with new eyes. German photographers in particular seemed determined to prove that God was a Cubist. More recently, following some years of Abstract Expressionism, evidence was forthcoming, via photomicrographs, that God was, instead, a pupil of Hans Hofmann. Both theories have merit, but why does the "proof" always follow the artistic event by about a decade. If Jackson Pollock had frequented the Massachusetts Institute of Technology I might think there was a connection between their graphs and his drippings. As it is, any relationship seems fortuitous and fruitless. Pollock's methods almost certainly grew out of his medium, out of an appreciation of spilled paint. The attempt, made repeatedly, to relate aerial survey photographs to abstractly patterned paintings is similarly far-fetched, a confusion of purposes and products. All that science has to offer art (or pattern) are the echoes of art's own abstractions.

The reason for giving the scientific and mechanical possibilities of pattern so much attention is that many people are infatuated with inventions and expedients. They see photographic texture as a panacea, not as the headache it often is. Since what the machine starts a man usually has to finish, I thought we might as well do our final Texture exercises by hand. Well, not entirely by hand; there are some ready-made ways of achieving texture which may be just what the modern decorator is looking for.

Again we visit an art or office-supply store to pick up some stencils or rubber stamps that will give good impressions of numbers or the letters of the alphabet. We will also need an inking pad for the stamps and a brush with short, stiff bristles for the stencils. What we want is to create textures without "texturizing;" textures made up not of specks or cryptic markings but of small solid shapes so crowded together and superimposed that their identity is merged. With conventional rubber stamps the effect will be limited to a texture-pattern on one ·plane, whether or not we have stamps of several sizes. Stencils are more promising. Before using them, I suggest we mix up a saucer of paint of each of several well-separated shades of grey, with our black construction paper as the darkest value, the white paper as the lightest. Beginning with the white ground, stencil the letters or numbers in the light grey, first, then the medium and the dark grey. If the impressions are well distributed and an equal amount of each grey is seen, we get an effect of light coming from behind the paper. On the black ground, reverse the order. Begin with the darkest grey and work towards the lightest to give, this time, an effect of depth or recession. Since these exercises will produce something approximating the sheets of texture we made in the last lesson, a matching unit of repeat can be made from them, as before, the new centers easily patched up with a bit of stamping or stencilling.

SEMI-MECHANICAL TEXTURES. Facing page top: NUMBERS. Bottom: LETTERS. Experiments in covering a surface with shapes made by stencil, from light to dark and from dark to light, respectively, as described above.

Texture, it will be clear by now, is a matter of multiplication. It can be made up of anything, natural or artificial, that will surrender its identity to a collective body. The use of the word "body" is deliberate; a texture should function, in a pattern, as part of a living organism. This can be a vital relationship or a dangerous one. As I noted before, the tendency of a texture to "take over" a pattern puts it in the class of a possible disfigurement. Texture defaces more patterns than it improves; it is never the answer to incompetence. But such is the power of proliferation that I see more and more separate objects being repeated, in close proximity, as if to force a pattern into existence by sheer numbers. This appears to be an approved method of pattern-making in some of the few schools that offer a course. We have seen, however that the additive method can work the other way. Separate images or objects, like our letters and numbers, can, through repetition, become so formless that they merely add up to a texture. There is nothing wrong about this, except for the fact that it is not a pattern. To me, the most delightful use of designing-by-addition occurs in certain style-conscious film titles and the animated short features by artists like Carmen d'Avino. Time is obviously an element in these creations but so is it in making a pattern and giving it texture. In both cases you must know when to stop.

Summary

No mechanical means for producing TEXTURE should be overlooked; some of them are more suitable for contemporary patterns than anything we can draw or paint. *The photographic processes should be investigated first, especially the use of various screens to give texture to solid images. A second series of exercises involves rubber stamps and stencils. Here the interest lies in creating textures, semi-mechanically, out of recognizable yet abstract shapes.* Still in a mechanical frame of mind, it is possible that the animated film, by building itself, bit by bit, gives us the best demonstration of TEXTURE—and, to some extent, of pattern making—we are likely to obtain.

DESIGN BY ADDITION. Facing page: THE FLOWERING. The culminating picture of an animated short made for Expo '67 by Carmen D'Avino. Tempera color on black paper. 1966. (Courtesy of the artist.) D'Avino is a painter who uses the motion picture screen as his canvas. In this subject the "story line" begins at the base of the stem and moves upward through a hundred-odd frames, branching out and blossoming as it goes. Animated film offers the artist-designer a two-fold delight. First, the color can have incredible luminosity, like sunlight shining directly through stained glass. Second, the audience can seem to participate in the artist's choice of embellishment: what he will do, and where. Very often a pattern designer wishes the various stages of his work could be experienced as he experienced them. Animation makes this possible, for each step is recorded on film. At the left-hand edge you may be able to see the marks M. D'Avino made for his camera as it moved up the paper. He worked to original music by Leonard Popkin.

COLOR

Lesson 1

The fourth and last element in pattern design is the one most people notice first. We, too, have been aware of Color since we began to turn shapes into patterns several lessons ago, but mainly it was to decide which areas should be light, which areas should be dark. "Chiaroscuro" is the western term for this disposition of light-and-dark tone values; the Japanese call the same thing *notan*. For true pattern makers a sense of the values of color takes precedent over color itself. Through many centuries of art, color played a comparatively minor role. It was either symbolic, or a decorative addition; paintings were essentially colored drawings. They were, nonetheless, carefully planned as to color: the light and dark areas were often underpainted with warm and cool neutral tones which the final colors—in their partial transparency—would utilize. So you see our own procedure has been historically sound. Such patterns as we have already made can be considered chiaroscuro sketches. If they have merit, color will enhance them, if they have not, it may lend them a superficial glamour. Two color-blind friends of mine only see black, white, and red—everything else is grey. It is all too easy to please them with predominantly red patterns; these, they say, agreeably "hurt" their eyes. My real successes are with patterns in colors they cannot distinguish, which they see as if photographed in black and white. When they admire these I know I have a product.

Criticism by the color-blind or the camera is beneficial because the average pattern will appear in from two to ten colorings, or colorways, as the trade calls them. To successfully undergo all these changes, a pattern must be legible from its inception. Had we broached the subject of Color too soon this legibility would have remained uncertain, for we would have beguiled and perhaps deceived ourselves by adding one pleasant color to another regardless of their light-and-dark values. As it transpired, Line led to Shape, shapes were seen to exhibit textures, and Texture, with its built-in depths of shade, went a long way towards establishing the requisite tonal system. Firmly based, we can confidently begin a high adventure with color.

To begin with, we rule out the notion of color "harmony." This is one of those concepts arising from a false analogy with music. Our color scale, although graded, bears no other resemblance to musical scales, and the "harmonies" we achieved through complementary, triad, and analogous—preferably called *adjacent* color schemes, for that's where they lie—are more accurately stated in terms of contrast and "support." I suppose the idea of absolute color harmony so popular in my youth, and still clung to in many textbooks, seemed justified by the rainbow. Certainly this is our spectrum, our prism, the content of our color wheel, but why must every color scheme try to encompass it? Were there no rainbows in Asia? If there were, the Chinese, Japanese, Siamese, Persians, and Indians could take them or leave them. The fact is that color preferences are local, and harmony—far from being objective—is the opinion of a group. Our time will best be spent in finding out how colors work.

No need to go deeply into theories. For our purpose, a color is known by the company it keeps. The comparison of one color with another begins with the difference between a warm grey and a cool grey; you were doubtless conscious of this difference when we confined ourselves to charcoal and marking pens, newsprint and construction paper, all of which have varying degrees of "temperature." When we use *paint* the differences become still stronger. Greys made from Ivory Black and white are quite unlike the greys made from Lamp Black and white; our whole study of color rests on such distinctions. *While it is necessary to know the standard colors, how to mix them, and how to modify them, you will always be handicapped as a colorist if you can't distinguish warm from cool.* The time to learn this is now. Make a tracing of one of your simpler patterns and execute it entirely in shades of what the French call *grisaille* and we call "beige" and "greige," playing one set of shades against the other. To several graded, standard greys, made with Ivory Black and white, add a small amount of Ochre Yellow for your warm shades (your beiges), and of Cobalt Blue for your cool shades (your greiges). In their paint dishes all the greys will look quite similar, but in juxtaposition, on the paper, they will develop intriguing casts of lavender and green, pink and tan. Josef Albers has named this phenomenon "interaction" and the term succinctly describes the effects of contrast, even between cold greys and warm greys where color is at a minimum.

Once rid of the obligation to create ideal harmonies, we can take a detached, truly objective view of the subject. Color, because of its emotional appeal, is the fashionable, not to say arbitrary, element that is added to pattern. We have seen how a conditioning to Texture took place; the same thing has happened, and much more openly, with Color. For nearly two decades I had observed that new color combinations first appeared in women's clothes; then it took several years before the decorators hailed them. This process has now become so accelerated that it must be obvious to everyone, including the proverbial man in the street. Only a few months after he sees his wife and daughters wearing strange bright colors, they are apt to appear among his household furnishings. Recall the successive popularity of pink-and-red, blue-and-green, pink-and-orange. A number of designers can claim a share in the acceptance of these combinations, but of late a more explicitly "oriental" palette has become common property, and almost obligatory. In the modern western world, I would say that it stems from the designs Leon Bakst made for Diagilev's Ballet Russe around 1910. Then there were many years when it seldom emerged except in the work of Matisse and a handful of his followers. Suddenly, after the second World War, and Korea, silks from Thailand were everywhere. Indeed it is still difficult to escape their pleasant, but insistent, exoticism—combining pink, magenta, and purple has become just too easy. A rare individual like Emilio Pucci, although brushed with the colors of our time, manages to keep his color schemes distinctive by exerting the strictest possible control of his tone values. A typical Pucci print combines four or five heightened pastels, relieved by light and dark accents. The routine colorist, seeking quick brilliance, uses too many saturated hues side by side: the effect is both shrill and monotonous.

pinkish mauve

*blue-lavender
(flowers
and basket)*

*light and deep
turquoise-green
(leaves)*

*rv. red-v-white
lines
(on mauve-colored
basket)*

*vermilion-red
(stems)*

THE CONTEMPORARY PALETTE. AT HOME COSTUME. Emilio Pucci. (Photograph courtesy the artist.) During the mid-sixties several tendencies in coloring combined and were given classic definition in the designs produced by Marchese Emilio Pucci Di Barsento of Florence, Italy. In this exquisite suit of silk-jersey "pajamas" we find the familiar analogous colors of Leon Bakst and Thailand, offset and clarified by expanses of oyster white. Clear shades of mauve and turquoise, with touches of sharp red, instead of being gaudy, are in effect heightened pastels—as perfectly balanced, in their values, as is the basket-and-flower motif in its surprising proportions.

Where do the fashion designers get their color inspiration? (Obviously, not all of it has come from southern Asia.) As a rule, the painters and the museums have supplied it, and the system has reached such efficiency that one can predict next season's "high fashion" colors by the nature of the major exhibitions. A designer scarcely needs to travel anymore; if he does, it is chiefly to dramatize a sales promotion. Meanwhile the catalogues and the publicity reach everyone in the designing profession. Throughout the world, designers who would not dream of ordering the *prix fixé* dinner at a restaurant "dine" on the same colors. Fortunately there always are, here and there, artists who reject pre-digested color schemes, along with whatever else has become hackneyed. Perhaps you have wondered at my continually calling attention to works of art, and to artists. This is why. Our debt is incalculable.

To escape standardization as much as we can, our Color Collection should be divided into two parts, one a file of reproductions, the other a scrap-book of collages and notes. You already know your favorite colorists among the moderns, but it would be a mistake to dismiss antiquity as being either garish or dun-colored. Although few complete painted color schemes of much interest to us remain from very ancient times—for the pigments were limited, or have not lasted—some of the backgrounds in the Roman frescos of southern Italy are unsurpassed for brilliancy and depth, and there is nothing in the world, even in a picture, like the iridescence of long-buried glass. Byzantine book illustration from the sixth through the tenth centuries offers another great experience, especially when the vellum was given a strong color, such as purple, beforehand, and the whole page raised to a pitch just short of luridness. The paintings I, personally, find irresistible, are panels from the early Renaissance where figures act out Biblical events in clear, candy-colored settings. A bit later a similar use of purely decorative color occurs in Indian, Persian, and Turkish miniatures. Then color becomes academic, subservient to drawing, until quite modern times.

But nothing will compare with the combinations you put together yourself. For years I have been picking up colored scraps along the street, or tearing pieces from magazines. This is the raw material for scrap-books on which I've spent many a relaxed hour trying one bit of colored stuff with another and pasting down what pleased me: In the same books—helter-skelter—are countless notations gleaned by observing passers-by, from shop windows, gallery exhibitions, and the theatre. "Pale blue grey, lemon, chocolate," "orange yellow, pinkish mauve, dried-blood red," may not sound like much, off-hand, but who can tell, when a specific problem arises, what marvels they might lead to?

Summary

It is wise to sneak up on COLOR—a subject which neither the text books nor the demands of fashion has exhausted. *The first distinctions we make are between warm and cool in an exercise where we mix various greys according to the instructions on page 149, and procede to paint a section of one of our own patterns.* Our Color Collection comes partly from art reproductions, partly from random scraps. *One of the best ways a designer can acquire a working knowledge of color is to fill small note books with collages of scraps and written notations of color schemes that catch his eye.* This is also a good way to circumvent the "oriental" formulae. We need a new rainbow.

Lesson 2

I am convinced that most people have a natural feeling for color which, in the name of education, has been jeopardized. See how readily primitive and untutored people achieve satisfactory color combinations; how self-consciously some of us do so. Books and magazine pieces on color are endless; a course on color is always popular. Where, then, did we lose a faculty which, I should think, is as naturally ours as a sense of equilibrium? One cannot hold the scientists entirely to blame. The physicist with his mixtures and measurements of light, the chemist with his studies of dyes and pigments are both valuable to us in numerous practical ways. Somewhat less so, to me, are the physiologist and the psychologist dealing with color. It is interesting to know how color is "perceived," but this has little bearing on how we will be using it. And the psychology of color, whatever its past fascination, is, nowadays, much ado about the obvious. Indeed, color becomes a useful tool only when we forget the laboratory and buckle down to work in the studio.

We assume that everyone knows that the *primary* pigments are Red, Yellow, and Blue, and that—presuming the purity of their hue—a *secondary* group, namely, Orange, Green, and Violet, can be made from them. In practice, designers, like painters (of all except the most realistic pictures), do less and less mixing of color. They learn the contents of about fifteen tubes or jars of paint and are thus able to produce whatever effects they want. For the colors just named are idealizations of the colors we actually buy; these, with few exceptions, differ from one manufacturer to another. A Crimson Red, a light Chrome Yellow, and an Ultramarine Blue can be considered the standard primaries in most cases, but it is best to purchase, along with your primary colors, the brightest secondary colors offered; otherwise you will get, by mixing your primaries, only dull versions of Orange, Green, and Violet. It is also wise to buy two other reds, a magenta and a burnt sienna; two other yellows, an ochre and a *medium* chrome yellow; and two other blues, a cobalt and a "mineral" blue. This brings our colors to a round dozen. Titanium White and Ivory Black are also required, and a medium warm grey is extremely convenient. In the brand of casein colors that I use (casein paints are water-soluble, but, on exposure, are waterproof, easily painted over, and non-fading) there are, in fact, five warm graded greys. But I only buy the middle one, the #3.

What do we do with these colors when we have them? We probe them. Almost any book on color will give you the necessary information about the Color Wheel, or Circle, and what to hope for when using it as a mixing guide. But precisely *what* each color does to another color *you will have to find out yourself with the particular brand of casein, tempera, or "designers'" colors you have chosen.* I use a fairly large kitchen crock for a water jar, cheap white china plates and saucers to mix my colors on, and old sheets for paint rags. My extravagance is brushes: square-tipped and pointed, broad and thin, bristle and sable, all with long handles. Buy a tablet of ordinary white watercolor paper and paint small sheets of it with uniformly strong color to make a color wheel of your own. It should have not less than twelve "spokes" if you want to test the purity of your pigments thoroughly.

You will notice that you don't need all fifteen tubes or jars of paint to produce a wheel. You will need them soon, however. Next, we begin exercises in matching colors; something a designer never stops doing. Did you get any nice color-combinations in those collages you made at the end of the last lesson? See if you can match them in paint. This is where your Black and White, your Ochre and Burnt Sienna will come in handy. And the color wheel itself. Today when we have such a marvelous array of prepared pigments at hand, the principal use of the color wheel is not as an aid to *producing* colors but to *modifying* them. Which is to say, making them warmer, cooler, or greying them down. These are, of course, relative matters, but generally speaking there is a warm and a cool side to the color wheel, with Red through Orange to Yellow on one side, and Violet through Blue to Green on the other. And any two colors, although neighbors, are warmer or cooler depending on their nearness to orange or blue—the poles of color temperature. This suggests the way adjacent, or related, colors can be modified, from one side or the other.

The greying or "toning down" of colors is another important function of the wheel. Black, and even White, can destroy the nature of a color, whereas modification by means of the complementary color—directly across the circle—will soften it, yet keep it alive and vibrant. White is like salt or sweetening, which our taste welcomes, but black is a pigment to be used, like pepper, with much caution. Added to yellows, black produces strange, wonderful greens; to orange, rich browns; to reds, lovely subtle violets. These are recipes—alchemies, really—it may take a little time to learn. *Meanwhile, do not forget the magic of greying with complementary colors.*

Grey, it would seem, is the quintessence of what color theorists mean by "harmony." (We might as well get this matter settled.) Johannes Itten, a teacher at the famed Bauhaus, states that "two or more colors are mutually harmonious if their mixture yields a neutral grey" and he quotes the physiologist Ewald Hering as saying "medium grey generates a state of complete equilibrium to the eye." This "grey," you understand, is not necessarily made of greyed colors; rather it is the sum total of whatever colors have been used—bright or dull. The theory, as I see it, is that when all the color vibrations have cancelled each other out we have perfect neutrality, perfect equilibrium.

That may be all right for pictures, for certain masterpieces. The reason I rejected, earlier, the whole concept of color harmony is that *patterns* are seldom colored according to rules, *nor do they claim to be a complete esthetic experience.* Itten's detailed examination of the "7 kinds of color contrast" is, for our purpose, much more to the point. Here he deals with ways to increase the brilliance of a color, and his discussion of "simultaneous contrasts" and "after-images," i.e., seeing complementary colors which are not actually present, should stimulate any artist. This is equally

TONE VALUES. Above: A Value Chart. If the abuse of bright color—at present so widespread—leads to another "beige age" such as we had in the forties, it will be more important than ever to visualize patterns in terms of their light-and-dark values. This chart has five values, from a light tone (which could be white), to a dark tone (which could be black). A novice designer will find it useful because five *values* are all that the average eye can distinguish in a sketch painted in monotone (or photographed in black and white), and five *colors* should be all he needs for an original pattern.

true of Faber Birren's studies. His analysis of the phenomena of iridescence and opalescence, for example, are most rewarding, and some of his proposals for "new uses of color" make one wish for another Salvador Dali, all skill, with nothing on his subconscious mind. Where I differ with the professional theorists of color is simply in doubting that "harmonies" can be prescribed.

Color, of all the four elements of pattern design, most needs to be played by eye. Every situation differs according to the scale, coverage, and other imponderables that go into a pattern; the only formula that invariably works is red, white, and gold for opera houses and circuses! To make colorways is an exhausting job. The top stylists are always falling back on black-and-white (they rediscover it every third or fourth season) and on the monochrome schemes, variations of a single hue, with which the production numbers in big musicals have made us as familiar as with the boy-and-girl misunderstanding at the end of the first act. Since new color combinations are quite irrational, our last exercise encourages them to be. When I teach design, I end the course by emptying out a bag of several hundred small pieces of fabric and paper, covering the vivid and the pastel, the greyed and the neutral colors as thoroughly as possible. The class then chooses partner/opponents and they present each other with two swatches of color that are (1) totally unrelated, (2) "swear at each other," or (3) are "too dull for words." The next move is for everyone to select, from the common stockpile, such colors as will turn the combination given him into an unusual yet satisfying scheme (which might, if the group indicated, be directed to a specific purpose, or a type of merchandise). Two or three additional colors are par, and it will soon be grasped that neutrals are seldom a solution, and that recourse to adjacent (or analogous) colors leads straight to banality.

What this informal contest amounts to is a new way of creating color combinations—"harmonies," if you insist. But as they are arrived at through deliberate discords or dullness, and made agreeable or even sensational by wholly intuitive means, I think they could best be described as *exercises in color acceptance*. The game is gratifying to everyone. As challengers, all players try to propose the next-to-impossible; as challenged, all players take pride in coming up with unexpected answers. When a successful solution is reached the unanimous approval is astonishing.

Summary

COLOR presents a curious paradox. In its application to that elusive thing called taste it can be intuited more easily than it can be explained. But our final exercises deal solely with the mixing and matching of paint. *First we make a color wheel to serve as a guide. Then we produce or match a number of colors, looking at the wheel to see what colors should be added.* These decisions are eventually made without thinking, although they follow definite rules. *Our eight lessons end in a little game (one or any number can play), which pushes color beyond the rules as they now exist.* If our appreciation of COLOR is as instinctive—or subconsciously conditioned—as it appears to be, might we not also instinctively know more about LINE, SHAPE, and TEXTURE than we thought we did? Learning, in the arts, consists mainly of bringing our feelings to the surface and making them tangible.

3

aspects
of
pattern

new documents for old

—A Designer's View

At some point, sooner or later, the question of originality arises. Just how original is an original pattern? In all honesty one must admit that the best of them—perhaps especially the best of them—are derivative, their dependence on other patterns quite apparent. If this were a creative period in the decorative arts, the intelligent use of the past would be taken for granted. A frank attitude towards "copying" is, in fact, the sign of a healthy tradition. Instead, during these eclectic times, too many designers are on the defensive with regard to originality, and never more so than when their sources are clearly visible. Magnified scale, trick printing, shock coloring, scrambled periods, are some of the ruses employed to give an illusion of freshness. Sometimes they succeed, and the results will be added to the fund of historical pattern that is always accruing. But the indications are that this, the third quarter of the twentieth century, will prove to be a time of indiscriminate borrowing when pattern designers tried everything and achieved little that endured.

Documentary patterns of the last several hundred years are a bonanza for everyone. Economically they are feasible, because a manufacturer need not pay for the time it takes to perfect them. Old patterns are not

NANCY McCLELLAND, VISIONARY. Facing page: BOUQUET. 18th century French wallpaper. Right: GEORGE WASHINGTON IN MASONIC TRIANGLE. American documentary wallpaper. Typical McClelland "finds," illustrating the range and character of this distinguished firm. (Photographs courtesy of Mary E. Dunn, President, Nancy Mc-Clelland, Inc.)

DEMURE AND REGAL ELEGANCE. Above: Raleigh Tavern. A fabric and a wallpaper made from a resist-printed cotton found at Colonial Williamsburg and imaginatively coordinated by reducing the scale of the paper and reversing its values. Fabric produced by F. Schumacher, wallpaper by Katzenbach and Warren. Facing page: Reception Room at Viscaya, Miami, Florida. These are the silk wall-panels Franco Scalamandré wove to replace the original panels made from Philippe de Lasalle designs for Marie Antoinette.

necessarily good patterns (and many barrels have been scraped) but as a rule a "document"—which is simply a record from the past—is apt to have design qualities that helped it to survive. These qualities are what guarantee the continuity of pattern, and it is foolish to rail against antiquarianism or commercialism, beyond noting that they often go hand in hand. Firmly established in the market place, traditional patterns, as they are called, escape the charges of "piracy" or flagrant copying (in trade jargon, "knocking off" a competitor's "line") that more original efforts must contend with. For this immunity we should demand the very highest quality.

Occasionally we get it. Nancy McClelland was a pioneer in the faithful reproduction of antique wallpapers, and some of her firm's imported papers continue to be printed from the original blocks, in France. But even the McClelland papers made in this country, by silk screen, are distinguished by their fidelity to their prototype, whether a scrap from a bandbox or the lining of a trunk. Faded grounds are matched meticulously, adding up to an inventory of hundreds of soft shades of almost incredible subtlety, and I understand that Miss McClelland made provisions for slightly off-register printing if the documentary suggested the same and she felt that it added charm.

Charm in greater quantities was offered by Katzenbach & Warren in 1938 with their initial collection of Williamsburg Wallpaper Reproductions. This was part of the first large-scale venture in licensing copies of decorative material from an American historical monument. It remains the strictest. A "museum" point of view was adopted from the beginning of the restorations at Colonial Williamsburg in the late twenties, using Rockefeller funds, and apparently there were many disputes between the various manufacturers and the trustees of the project over authenticity versus saleable merchandise. No matter how drab the existing document, it had to be reproduced exactly. Thereafter some leeway was allowed in developing several other color schemes, or "colorways," provided they fell within the cheerful but rather limited palette that research had revealed as being typical of the period. Further relaxation was allowed in the category of "commemorative" subjects, put together from early sources such as drawings, but here too the aim was versimilitude. A commemorative design had to look as though it might have existed at the time. Good copies are so easily made in wallpaper—even when printed by machine for the mass market—that it is discouraging to find some of the larger firms claiming authenticity for their patterns after they have

DOCUMENTARY INGENUITY. Facing page: SHELL TOILE. Fifty-inch wide fabric made by Brunschwig et Fils, New York, from pattern on the narrow printed early 19th-century French cotton shown above. (Photographs courtesy of Mrs. Murray Douglas, Vice President, Brunschwig et Fils, Inc.) The original toile was supplied with a missing feather at the right side — among other things. This is an excellent example of reconstruction, because, to get a perfect match within the prescribed width of the new material, all the motifs had to be shifted slightly and then redrawn to the crispness of the original engraving.

"Good grief, Marge! Not my pajamas, too!"

taken the two routine liberties with the originals: changing their scale and "texturizing" (an ugly word for the ugly habit of faking texture) them beyond recognition.

Fabrics, on the whole, receive more sensible reproduction. Since cloth possesses actual texture and need not imitate it, and a fabric that looks "old" also looks shabby, manufacturers try to make modern equivalents rather than slavish copies. Or some of them do. The leader in this field, in America, is Franco Scalamandré, his fine Italian hand evident in everything his firm, specializing in reproductions of antique silks, makes. Scalamandré started out as an instructor in mathematics at Naples, working with various textile mills on their technical problems. He came to America in 1924, and by 1928 had formed his own company which at first dealt in imported materials. Then William Randolph Hearst asked him if he could copy an old damask, and so, with a single loom in a rented room in New Jersey, the success story began. As I write, the scores of Jacquard looms in Mr. Scalamandré's mills in New York and Italy have produced the fabrics for nearly three hundred historical buildings, in-

HOME DECORATING VICTIM. Drawing by Robt Day. (Courtesy *The New Yorker.*)

cluding many palaces and the White House. Sometimes the fabrics are an outright gift, being of a quality the available money could not buy. The engineer in Franco Scalamandré cannot resist a fantastically difficult assignment if it also promises to satisfy the artist in him. Sixty-eight thousand Jacquard punch-cards were required for the Palm Tree panels at Mr. James Deering's great Renaissance-styled residence "Viscaya," in Miami, (now a museum) and each of the eighteen panels took two months to weave.

Translating old patterns into new fabrics demands skill, patience, and taste. The document is often no more than a crumbling fragment; a repeat may have to be invented and the whole unit imperceptibly rescaled to conform to the widths of material in current use. In the studio of Brunschwig & Fils, New York, all these intricate operations are endlessly performed by Joan Kaminski and her assistants under the supervision of Mrs. Zelina Brunschwig. No amount of care in reactivating a pattern is too great for this fastidious firm. Here the emphasis is on eighteenth-century French and English prints, generally rendered in variations of the original color schemes but sometimes boldly updated. When vibrating colors are used, the stepping-up is done gradually. "Mrs. B"'s special love is exquisite drawing and she is aware that unless the original sequence of light-and-dark tone values is maintained the fine draftsmanship can be lost in chaos.

The above, and perhaps a dozen other firms stick closely to their originals, mostly French, English, and American documents for printed fabrics and wallpaper, Italian and French ones for woven fabrics. "Eighteenth century" is a magic phrase as far as American decorators are concerned. Their infatuation with the patterns of that time, and the knowledge that they were used for a variety of purposes, has encouraged the duplication of a single pattern on both fabrics and wallpaper, beginning with the older patterns and extending to contemporary designs. We know that fabric was used on walls before paper was, but the blotting out of an entire background is unprecedented. If this mania for matching continues, it will undoubtedly include floorcovering. Then, surely, it will be advisable to use different scales for different materials, in addition to a smaller scale for the wallpaper—to create distance—as I have long advocated. A few manufacturers have on occasion reversed the values of paper and fabric (printing the motif of one, the ground of the other, to give a semblance of two planes) but I am told the public has never been receptive to the idea. A complete duplication of color as well as size is still considered essential for a "decorator look," regardless of whether the room resembles a mill-end shop or a jungle.

Museums are a designer's usual source of documents, although, due to the culture explosion and the drain upon museum personnel, the museum of today appears to be a house divided: a place of entertainment—a haven for scholars. A serious designer, respecting these functions, soon becomes frustrated. Sketching and photographing in American museums is habitually frowned upon, yet the photographic files in most institutions are neglected, and to expect help from preoccupied curators is out of the question. At the Brooklyn Museum Design Laboratory, catering to the demand for documents and assistance has become a business. Individuals or companies pay an annual fee for a membership that carries many privileges. These benefits include access to an enormous file of "swatches" and textile pattern-books that go back to 1770, consultation periods re-

garding special needs, and even freedom to borrow actual objects from the museum's collections. Dorothy Tricario, the Fashion and Textile Co-ordinator, says that hundreds of designers use their facilities and services on a yearly basis, "generally working from an idea to a product." In the course of developing an idea she may bring anything from beaded bags to totem poles to the designer-client's attention. And the product in mind may range from lingerie to automobile upholstery.

On his own, a designer uses documents somewhat less dramatically. If he is doing a job of "editing" he will want to retain a period appearance, however much he pulls the motifs apart, eliminates some of them, and adds other motifs. This is in line with modern practice and the results can be admirable. If, on the other hand, a designer uses an ornamental motif or a repeating scheme simply as a point of departure, he may not think it necessary to reveal the historical source. Nor is it. We know that all patterns are based to some degree on other patterns—we don't care where Shakespeare found his plots, only what he made from them. Still, it is commendable, and often wise, for a designer to be open in his borrowings. First, giving credit where credit is due is a mark of integrity. Second, to copy conscientiously is to learn. Third, learning leads to creating. That, briefly, was the apprentice system, for which the commercial design studio of today may, with reservations, be considered a substitute.

Notable pattern designs that may well become documents of tomorrow are often created by designers of marked originality who are also active in other areas. The gifted pattern designer Ilonka Karasz is well known for her *New Yorker* magazine covers, and James Reynolds has made a reputation as a writer of books on architecture and Irish ghosts. Today, many outstanding pattern makers, although as dissimilar as Leoda da Mar, the Tillets, the "Ellenhanks," Jack Denst, and the author, are man-ufacturers of patterned materials as well as designers. The question we asked in the beginning echoes and re-echoes: "How original is an original pattern?" When does it warrant a signature? The great patterns of the past were—or seem to be—anonymous, the fruit of many talents. No one knows better than a professional designer what his sources are and the degree of his own contribution. Claiming originality is an ethical prob-lem. How it is solved is up to the individual.

FASHION. Right: MANTEAU BY WORTH. Ca. 1890. (In the Brooklyn Museum Collection.) Facing page: Detail espe-cially photographed for this book by Wolfgang R. Hartman. Many large museums have costume collections and they are always worth a visit.

The entanglement of past and present also involves the *decorator*. Eclecticism is nothing new; it becomes noticeable whenever there are more influences than the tastemakers of the time can absorb. Under these circumstances the temptation to pile pattern, pell-mell, on pattern—trusting that the "law of profusion," mentioned earlier, will work—must be overwhelming. Yet it should be resisted. And although I hope we will be spared a return to strictly period rooms (too often eked out with imitations), there is much to be said for rooms that have a dominant character and conjure up the emotion that goes with a specific time or place. The part that pattern can play in such a setting is tremendous. But it needs to be played with discernment quite as much as with flair. If decorators do not set up standards for the selection and use of pattern, who will?

PATTERN ON PATTERN. Left: TAPESTRY PANEL. Detail. Eastern Mediterranean. (Courtesy, Museum of Fine Arts, Boston. Charles Potter Kling Fund.) Facing page: SITTING ROOM IN DARK HARBOR, MAINE, SUMMER HOME OF MRS. HENRY PARRISH II. (Reprinted from *House & Garden*; Copyright © 1966 by the Condé Nast Publications, Inc.) Combinations of patterns have been a testing-ground of taste through the centuries, and certainly one plays safe to restrict them. But the fragment on the left, while disconcerting, is both literally and artistically held together by two stripes, and the Parrish sitting room is a resounding triumph for "the law of profusion," American style. The walls are light blue, most of the fabrics are in strong colors on light grounds, and all colors used are gathered together in the large rag rug.

‡ 3 *Bellis minor prolifera.*
Childing Daiſie.

4 *Bellis minor ſylueſtris.*
The ſmall wilde Daiſie.

5 *Bellis media ſylueſtris.*
The middle wilde Daiſie.

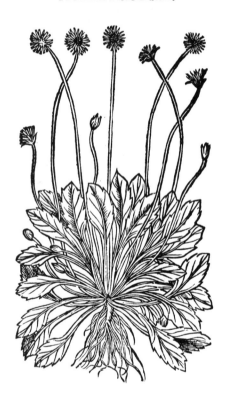

thoſe of the common Daiſie, of a darke green colour : among which comes vp a fat ſtem ſet round abont with the like leaues, but leſſer. The floures grow at the top globe-faſhion, or round like a ball, of a perfeƈt blew colour, very like vnto the floures of mountain Scabious.

  7   The French blew Daiſie is like vnto the other blew Daiſies in each reſpeƈt, ſauing it is altogether leſſe, wherein conſiſteth the difference.

‡   There were formerly three figures and deſcriptions of this blew Daiſie, but one of them might haue ſerued ; for they differ but in the talneſſe of their growth, and in the bredth and narrowneſſe of their leaues.   ‡

¶ *The Place.*
The double Daiſies are planted in gardens : the others grow wilde euery where.

the handpainted soapbox
——William Morris

On the 24th of March, 1834, at Walthamstow, Essex, England, a hero was born. Few people in his lifetime knew he was a hero because he was also a prominent poet, a successful designer and manufacturer of decorative art goods, a radical politician, and a printer of fine books who collected rare ones. These were not separate guises. The most disconcerting thing about William Morris is that his varied talents and interests, together with his inconsistencies, blind spots, and weaknesses, add up to a single figure of genius. Well-to-do and full of energy, what he could have been is a great dilettante: he left no masterpieces to prove he was not. Neither could his ideas, in themselves, be called original. His obsessive medievalism and much of his Socialism stemmed from Ruskin; his decorative subjects were the common property of the Pre-Raphaelite school of painters. J. W. Mackail's *The Life of William Morris,* first published in 1899, three years after Morris died, informs us that the poetry Morris began writing at the age of twenty-one, at Oxford, struck astonishment from his friends. That it should have is what would astonish many people today. Morris himself expressed surprise during most of his life at the ease with which he wrote rhymes, and this may be the reason he exclaimed to Burne-Jones near the end of his life, "Poetry is tommy-rot." But he was naturally in no position to see that his poems—for all their banality and ease—had made him what he was. They were his stepping-stones, his talismans.

A poetic temperament is common to the young, who are inquisitive and ardent. Delicate health can be an advantage. Mackail quotes Morris's mother as saying repeatedly, "He had to be kept alive by calve's feet jelly and beef tea," but even so, by the age of five he was deeply immersed in the Waverly novels of Sir Walter Scott. As if reading them were not enough, when he was six years old the family moved from an edge of

WOODCUT AND VARIATIONS. Facing: A page from *The Herbal, or General History of Plantes* by John Gerard, London, 1597. (Photograph courtesy the Rare Book Room of the Central Public Library, New York.) Above: DAISY. 1864. Below: LILY. 1873. Two wallpapers by William Morris. There is no question of Morris "copying" Gerard, but it is clear that the *Herbal* made a deep impression on him, and, like most artists, Morris, in the "Lily," did recall his "Daisy" pattern of nine years before. But, although it is less crowded, the sprays of leaves in the "Lily" provide a less suitable background for low-growing plants than the grasses of the earlier work.

Epping Forest into its depths. There, in what Mackail describes as "a large spacious mansion of Georgian date, standing in about fifty acres of park," he and his four brothers rode their ponies around the park (William, in a little suit of armour) and into the forest, where they hunted rabbits and small birds. The forest was exceptional for its dense thickets of pollarded hornbeams that cast a profound shade even on the brightest days. Morris had his own garden in the park, Gerard's *Herbal* illustrated with wood-cuts in the house; and so, what with the adjacent forest, he was early imbued with a love of flowering verdure, which he would later discover in Gothic tapestries. A love of Gothic architecture was likewise instilled in the child by visits with his father to Canterbury and other churches. When he went off to Marlborough College, at not quite fourteen, he had grown strong in body and was possessed with "an extraordinary eye and even more extraordinary memory." Mackail insists that "no landscape, no building that he had once seen did he ever forget, or confuse with another." What a schoolfellow at Marlborough remembers is "a thick-set, strong-looking boy, with a high color and black curly hair, good-natured and kind, but with a fearful temper."

At Exeter College, Oxford, where Morris was studying with the expectation of taking Orders, Edward Jones (later, Edward Burne-Jones), who was also studying for Orders and who was to be Morris' closest friend throughout his life, gave him the name of Topsy. His dark mop of hair and somewhat unkempt appearance never changed. Although at about

POINT OF DEPARTURE. Above: VICTORIAN RUG PATTERN. Morris is said to have been so horrified by the products of England's mid-19th century industrial revolution that he refused to attend the Great Exhibition extolling it, in 1851, when he was seventeen years old. Ornamental mishmash, such as that pictured, is what led Morris to base his early patterns on fresh observations of nature.

this time Morris came of age and into "something like L 900 a year," none of his friends realized his fortunate circumstances unless they visited his home during a vacation. All six or seven of the "set," as these friends first called themselves, were Anglo-Catholics, avid readers of Carlyle and Tennyson as well as the almost-required John Ruskin, with other interests divided between social reform and plain-song. Out of this melange, when they had presently come to refer to themselves as "the Brotherhood," grew *The Oxford and Cambridge Magazine, conducted by members of the two Universities,* in spite of the fact that no one from Cambridge wrote for it, and all the expenses were born by Morris alone. It lasted for exactly one year, then was discontinued as the "brothers" interests diverged still further.

Burne-Jones, meanwhile, had met Dante Gabriel Rossetti, a poet and the most flamboyant of the Pre-Raphaelite group of painters, who was to have such an inordinate influence on William Morris. There are some lines by Rossetti paraphrasing Sappho, which go, "Like the sweet apple that reddens/atop on the topmost bough/atop on the topmost twig/which the pluckers forgot somehow. Forgot it not, but got it not/for none could get it till now," that have a mesmerizing quality the man himself must have exerted. Partly under Rosetti's spell, first Burne-Jones then Morris decided not to take Orders, and when they left Oxford together Jones at once began his career as a painter while Morris struggled for nearly a year in an architect's office. Gradually Rossetti took both their destinies in hand, and for two more rather miserable years Morris tried to become a painter and only succeeded in becoming a patron of painting. According to Mackail, "Rosetti, now as always perfectly unscrupulous in his means towards an end he believed to be of primary importance, probably did not look beyond the immediate interests of his own art. For him, at the time, English society was divided into two classes. The duty of one class was to paint pictures . . . The duty of the other class was to buy the pictures." In short, it was a division which put Morris on both sides, a position he was to become accustomed to.

Nothing is lost on an artist. After architecture had rejected him, and while painting was in the process of doing so, Morris found himself on the threshold of a new career that combined something of each. He and Burne-Jones had taken unfurnished studio lodgings in Red Lion Square, London; when they could find nothing in the shops to their liking, Morris designed, and engaged a carpenter to make, what Rossetti was pleased to call "intensely medieval furniture, tables and chairs like incubi and succubi." There was also a huge settle with cupboards above, that Rosetti, long a familiar of spirits and demons, did not hesitate to decorate with painted allegories. This formidable piece of furniture was later set up in the drawing room at Red House, Bexleyheath, Kent, as part of the extensive decorations that Morris and his friends executed for the house he and the architect Philip Webb planned and built in anticipation of Morris's marriage to Jane Burden. Out of these activities, the firm of "Morris, Marshall, Faulkner & Co., Fine Art Workmen in Painting, Carving, Furniture, and the Metals" was a logical growth. Formed along partnership lines in April, 1861, with a working capital of only slightly over L 100, it continued until March, 1875, with William Morris supplying most of the initiative, money as needed, and labor. Whenever Rosetti, Ford Maddox Brown, Webb, Burne-Jones or the several other members of the loosely-conceived firm were called upon to supply a design they

were promptly paid for it. Faulkner, a good friend since "Brotherhood" days had also proved to be a good manager. But in order to continue, the firm must expand, and this made the less dedicated members apprehensive, since they would be liable for any debts incurred. Now they demanded their share of the L 8000 the company was estimated to have earned over a fourteen year period. Morris again dug in his pockets, and Rosetti, whose friendship had become an exasperation to Morris (al-

DESIGNER AT WORK. Above: EVENLODE. William Morris. 1883. Sketch for a chintz seen in full repeat on the facing page. (The Victoria & Albert Museum, London.) "Evenlode" came at the beginning of what Peter Floud (1912-1960) authoritatively marked out as Morris's Third Period. At that time the "V.&A."—then known as the South Kensington Museum—had just acquired a piece of 15th-century Italian cut velvet, and its diagonal composition prompted Morris to use diagonals and meandering verticals in striking ways of his own. Many of the seventeen patterns of this period have subsidiary motifs moving against the main motif, and all of them are rich in invention.

172

though not, it seems, to his wife), finally disappeared from the circle. Morris & Company went on, with Burne-Jones, Webb, and Faulkner faithfully attached to it, and other talents gravitating to it through the years, but it was, nevertheless, essentially a one-man business.

Essentially, too, it was what we would call an interior decorating firm, with Morris the contact man and head salesman. It is a bit troubling to think of him on the boat to Ireland or the train to Scotland to show his chintzes to a countess. He had designed them, he had prepared the dyes, and he had virtually printed them, now he must take the measurements for upholstery and draperies! He considered this part of his job. When figuring yardage for a room at St. James' Palace he was as unselfconscious as when he was dipping skeins in the large, buried vats of dye that kept his forearms stained an indigo blue for months on end. Was he not a workman? Most of Morris's associates regarded his Socialism with sadness, but as he was elected an Honorary Fellow at Oxford on the same day he chose to formally join the notoriously liberal Democratic Federation, I would have thought his friends were aware, by then, of his need for latitude and his love of contradiction. There was his restless energy as well. It was recalled by companions of undergraduate days that Morris "had a habit of beating his own head, dealing himself vigorous blows, to take it out of himself." To take what out?

Creative persons know that anyone working in the arts must have obstacles. If circumstances do not provide them, the artist must. Possessed of great vitality and some money (although the fortune his father had made in copper was gone) Morris handicapped himself with duties and diversions which, it was generally agreed, were sufficient for ten ordinary men. There was the Society for the Protection of Ancient Buildings; this took up much time, over the years, and cost him many commissions when he flatly decided that the stained glass windows he and Burne-Jones created were unsuited for restorations. There was his prolonged study of the Icelandic language and two voyages to Iceland to visit the birthplace of the Sagas he had spent years in rewriting. There was his mastery of the art of dyeing, and of weaving tapestries and rugs, in addition to all the experiments necessary for printing on cloth. Finally there were the translations from the Iliad and the Odyssey, besides four or five volumes of original poetry and the complicated task of moving his manufacturing operations from London to Merton Abbey. It may have been with relief that William Morris turned to politics and mounted what I have presumed to call—intending no disparagement—his handpainted soapbox.

Designers face a continual dilemma. Their work is specialized and

INSPIRATION AND RESULT. Facing page top: Brocaded Silk. Colors and gold threads on a ground of silver tissue. Venetian. First half of the 16th century. Bottom: Rose and Lily. William Morris. 1880. (Both fabrics: The Victoria & Albert Museum, London.) Morris's reputed adaptation of the Venetian pattern, top, scarcely improved it. At pains to eliminate the crowns, he replaced them with a poorly drawn rose, and the rose leaves he introduced along the ogee framework are a further, unnecessary distraction.

technical, yet to do good work they must see it in a large context and have the most passionate convictions about it. Morris was not lacking in these. He was only seventeen at the time the 1851 Exhibition glorified England's new industrial age, but already he was filled with revulsion by anything of a shoddy appearance. Later, painting under Rossetti's spell, he found that he could do one thing, at least, superbly: the purely decorative parts of his pictures anticipate the nearly six hundred pattern and ornamental designs which were to constitute his major work. That is to say, Morris's best poetry is not in his poems but in his patterns. Where the rhymes of the one barely avoid doggerel, the repetitions of the other reach lyrical grandeur. I think he knew this. After he had read his first poem aloud to the Oxford "set" and all hailed it as an extraordinary accomplishment, he remarked, "Well, if this is poetry, it's very easy to write,"—something he never felt about pattern designing, which he called a "harassing business."

Paradoxically, it was his visual experiences rather than his literary ones that he wished to share. It is typical of him that during the dozen years he was most politically minded (roughly from 1877 to 1890) his continuing concern was to inculcate the working man with a desire for the life beautiful. We do not know what Morris preached on hundreds of wet, windy streetcorners during his most active years, 1884 and 1885, but in the printed text of a number of talks before predominately labor audiences he seemed to be trying to open their eyes, particularly to their own surroundings. Not one of them could have afforded a length of his fabrics or even a roll of his "paper-hangings," yet in his overwhelming need to communicate with them—not as individuals, but as a class—he would discuss the qualities a good pattern ought to have! Because that is what he knew best. It is fascinating to read these lectures Morris gave, often in small dingy meeting rooms, and imagine the expressions on the men's faces when they heard such Ruskin-like axioms as, "Have nothing in your homes that you do not know to be useful, or believe to be beautiful," and, "No work which cannot be done with pleasure in the doing is worth doing." One wonders if Morris was not patronizing his listeners. More likely it was the other way around.

When Morris stepped down from his soapbox, Mackail ventures to suggest that the long public struggle to reconcile Art and Socialism as they existed in a mythical Middle Ages not only broke down his health but "to an extent wore away the keen edge of his mind." Nearly every task he undertook had contained contradictions. He himself was a living anachronism, a twelfth-century man with a romantic message for a world fast becoming mechanical. The archaisms in his fictional writing were intended to conjure up happier, simpler days, but merely made him hard to read. Since he never compromised the quality of the things he produced (and this was his quite legitimate objection to using machines for certain processes) only persons of some means could afford them. A similar criticism could be made of the entire Arts and Crafts movement, much of which is credited to Morris because of his pioneer cooperation with other artist-artisans at Red House many years before. His final self-indulgence—the Kelmscott Press, named for his beloved garden home on the upper Thames—would seem absurdly precious if we did not know the trouble he went to: the long search for vellum, the meticulous design of two type faces. None of his public crusades are so moving as the artistic perfection he sought in private. And this is nowhere more evident than in the seventy-six pattern designs he invented over a period of thirty-two years.

Peter Floud (1912-1960) made the most thorough examination of Morris's repeating patterns that we possess, and I am pleased to recount his findings before adding a few observations of my own. Mr. Floud tells us that the first three wallpapers that Morris produced in 1864—the Trellis, the Daisy, and the Fruit, or Pomegranate—should be regarded as experimental since they are not typical of his work in what Floud calls "the four mature periods," from 1872, when he began pattern designing "for serial production" again, to the year of his death in 1896. The nine papers and the three printed textiles in the First Period, 1872-1876, are, like the three listed above, quite naturalistic in their general effect. This was in distinction to the cheaper, abjectly realistic Victorian designs then available, and to the rather formal patterns by the Gothic Revival "establishment": Pugin, Owen Jones, and the others. Some confusion is inevitable here. At an exhibition in Paris in 1882 Morris's Sunflower paper won a gold medal for "exactness of imitation" of medieval work, whereas the designer himself considered all of his work thoroughly modern, although inspired by the Middle Ages. During the prolific Second Period, 1876-1883, with eleven wallpapers and thirty-two chintzes, a rigid "Gothic" look is undeniable. As Peter Floud explains it, Morris was preoccupied with weaving at this time, and it is usual for woven patterns to be symmetrical around a vertical axis. In the Third Period, from 1883 to 1890, greater freedom and originality return. A piece of fifteenth-century Italian cut velvet just acquired by the South Kensington Museum (as the Victoria & Albert was then called) provided Morris with a diagonal construction for nine out of the seventeen patterns in this group; also for new ways to conventionalize his foliage and flowers. The Fourth Period, 1890-1896, coincides with Morris's intensive activities at his Kelmscott Press: fifty-two publications in six years! In the last ten wallpapers and a single design for chintz, diagonals are replaced by an undulating upward movement, often with subsidiary motifs. Peter Floud finds it unfortunate that Morris never entirely recovered the fluidity of the First Period, that from 1878 onwards his studies of historical fabrics made him stress structure above naturalness. The irony here, as Floud's one-time assistant Barbara Morris (no relation) pointed out to me, is that the fabrics he studied were not, as he thought, Gothic, but transitional to the Renaissance period he detested.

To a designer, the hallmark of all the Morris patterns is a profusely covered surface. They share this with the Victorian period as a whole, and it is amazing that Morris was able to achieve such a variety of appearances while retaining almost uniformly dense coverage. That he was

THE FOUR PERIODS. Overleaf: On the next four pages are examples of the phases Morris went through as a pattern designer, following Peter Floud's chronology. (1-5, Courtesy of The Victoria & Albert Museum, London.) 1, WILLOW (1874), represents the naturalism of the First Period very well, although 2, ACANTHUS (1875), has a formal quality closer to the Second Period. 3, BOWER (1877), at the beginning of the Second Period, shows formality creeping in, and 4, THE STRAWBERRY THIEF (1883), shows it in all its symmetry. 5, CRAY (1884), top of page 180, is a good example of the dynamic Third Period. 6, COMPTON (1896), left, page 181, brings the Fourth Period to a close, summing up as it does the best qualities of each period.

1. THE VICTORIA & ALBERT MUSEUM, LONDON.

2. THE VICTORIA & ALBERT MUSEUM, LONDON.

3. THE VICTORIA & ALBERT MUSEUM, LONDON.

4. THE VICTORIA & ALBERT MUSEUM, LONDON.

5.   THE VICTORIA & ALBERT MUSEUM, LONDON.

MASTER AND DISCIPLES. Above and facing page: CRAY, above, and COMPTON, facing page, left, are unmistakably Morris, but what about the pattern facing page, right—GOLDEN LILY (1899) by J. H. Dearle? (Photograph courtesy of Arthur Sanderson & Sons Ltd., London.) According to a bulletin from the William Morris Society, of which R. C. H. Briggs, Kew, Surrey, England, is Honorary Secretary, "The firm of William Morris & Company, Decorators, Ltd., sold about one hundred different designs of wallpapers, including ceiling papers. Of these, William Morris designed 52. The remainder were the work of J. H. Dearle, Miss May Morris, Miss Kate Faulkner, Miss Kersey and Mr. W. A. S. Benson." To clear up "instances of confusion between wallpaper designs by Morris himself and other members of the firm" the bulletin lists all such patterns, based on a catalogue put out in 1909. What to me is so remarkable is the uniformly high quality in the work of his pupils—as I have seen it in the comprehensive Joseph Dunlap collection here in America. Morris taught well.

180

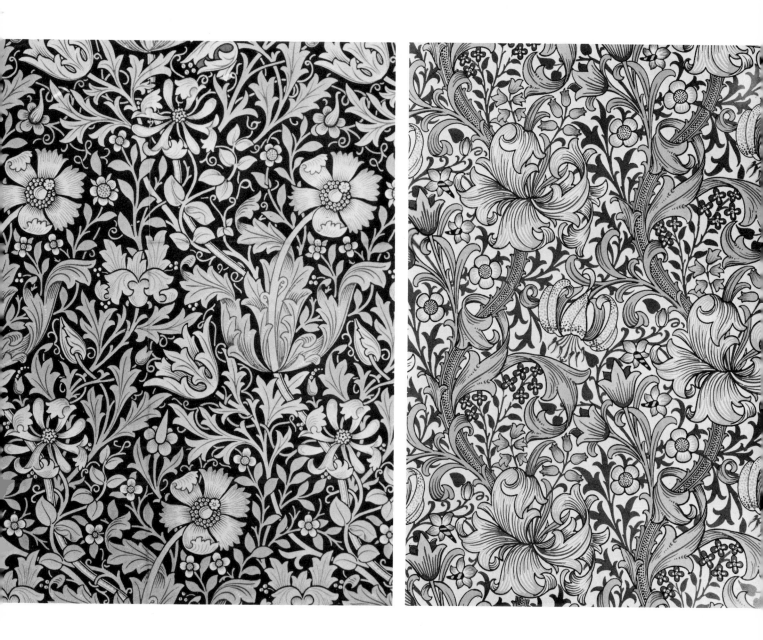

is due to his sense of architectural structure and scale, combined with a poet's references to nature even in the stiff patterns of the Second Period. He passed these aptitudes on to his pupil and successor, J. H. Dearle, whose patterns, now and again, almost seem superior to those by Morris, like a skillful job of editing. But in Compton, the last design Morris made, a few months before his death, all his virtuosity and grace is gathered up in one unending bouquet. On the rainy morning they buried him from Kelmscott there were mourners from several social levels. Each said farewell to a different person. Perhaps only Ned Burne-Jones, standing at the foot of the grave, knew all the men Morris had been, and even he might not have seen the pattern that held his great lonely friend together.

182

a class by themselves
——Bizarre Silks

Few traits are so deeply ingrained in us as curiosity. The pull of the unknown was as strong in Alexander the Great as it apparently is in the astronauts. While the methods and the directions of travel change, little else does. Horace Greeley advising "Go West, young man" a hundred years ago spoke for his time and place. Four centuries earlier Columbus had sailed West in hopes of reaching the East. Many voyages are undertaken, or said to be undertaken, like conquests, strictly for gain; but what does anyone actually hope for, from the moon or the ink-dark depths of the sea? It is new experiences we are always seeking; fame and fortune, if they come, are by-products, frequently delayed and quite different from what might have been expected. Alexander, reaching Gandhara (now western Pakistan) in 327 B.C. could not have guessed that his visit would be responsible for the peerless school of Roman-styled sculpture that would flourish there—using Buddhist subject-matter—four hundred years later. Nor, except for the artists who followed in his wake, would it have existed. Today war, science, industry, commerce, and art are so intertwined as to seem dependent on each other. But in earlier times the trade in rare commodities and the subsequent art forms developed more slowly, almost as if they grew out of sailor's souvenirs.

At least that is the way, by most accounts, the East-West trade started up, all over again, and on a much larger scale, during the sixteenth century. Charles McKew Parr in his *Jan Van Linschoten, The Dutch Marco Polo* uses diaries and official reports to tell of the frightful journeys around the Cape of Good Hope and how a young Hollander named Jan, shipping first with the Portuguese, learned their routes and their diplomacy, and so helped his own country to wrest the East Indian trade away from Portugal. Yet no amount of maritime knowledge could lessen the hazards of storms, piracy, epidemics, and scurvy. Greed alone could not have driven men to make a voyage during which half the crew would die; each trip reads like the horrible romance of men in love with strangeness. Barter was a dividend. Super-cargoes—as the officers in charge of

"...THE SLIGHTLY OBSCENE SHAPES, THE IMPROBABLE FLOWERS."
Facing page: Author's sketch of detail from PART OF A PALAMPORE, Indian cotton, 17th-18th century, in *Bizarre Designs in Silks* by Vilhelm Slomann, published by Ejnar Munksgaard, Copenhagen. Is this how the silks "in a class by themselves" began?

merchant ships were called—could bring back merchandise on their own, and seemingly the crew did too. Many ships sank simply from being overloaded.

Such is our background. If one reads about the Goncourt brothers, Edmond and Alfred, and their artistic circle in the Paris of the eighteen-seventies and -eighties one thinks of the exoticism of that era as being soft, precious, and just a bit silly. A friend of the Goncourts, the great Gustave Flaubert, referred to his own novel *Salammbô as* "a feast of historical hashish" (others, it is said, dropped the last three letters of hashish). Yet despite the theatrical warehouse atmosphere of *Salammbô* I recall Flaubert's description of an evening fete in the palace gardens at Carthage when torches set the palm trees on fire, and huge apes, in flames, fell out of them screaming. It is barbaric images such as this that I glimpse, rightly or wrongly, behind the interminable transactions of the four East India Companies, down to and including the later periods when oriental curiosities in general were known as chinoiserie. Few things are prettier or more quaint than objects made "in the Chinese taste." Few things have (for me) more violence behind their delicate appearance. Our immediate subject—a group of fabrics woven in silk and metal threads, roughly between 1695 and 1710—brings these two qualities uniquely together. Not without reason are they called "Bizarre," their motifs described as "enigmatic."

They did not have a name until fifteen or so years ago. In 1953 Dr. Vilhelm Slomann published a book entitled *Bizarre Designs in Silks*. Translated from Danish and printed in English in Copenhagen, Dr. Slomann's provocative work was based, according to his preface, on an exhibition held at the Danish Museum of Decorative Arts in 1935. This exhibit consisted of silk textiles from half-a-dozen European museums, together with painted and printed cottons from the George P. Baker collection, now in the Indian section of the Victoria & Albert Museum. Its avowed purpose was to "attempt to throw light on the problem relating to the bizarre designs in silks"—although, at that time, they were nameless. Most of the silks appear to have come from Scandinavian or German institutions; the same is true of the photographs in the Slomann book. Almost without exception he refers to the many plates as being an "Indian pattern; about 1700," and one of the first questions that arises is how so many Indian-type patterns were either produced, found their way, or came to be treasured so far north. Dr. Slomann expresses gratitude for having seen photographs of fantastic silk patterns in American collections (for instance) but mostly prefers to draw upon examples nearer home. Being of Dutch descent I understand the Northerner's passion for exotica.

The Dutch East India Company was founded in 1602, the Danish East India Company in 1614. Is one to infer that—a hundred years later—the ships of these two countries brought their choicest Indian fabrics directly to Holland, Germany, and Scandinavia? It would almost appear so. However, the Slomann theory, which, in brief, sought to prove that his "Indian patterns" not only derived their motifs from India, but were woven there, is viewed with some scepticism. Like William Goodyear's 1891 theory of the lotus motif as being the source of everything decorative from the Ionic capital to the acanthus scroll, it goes too far. On page 45 of Dr. Slomann's book he shows "Part of a Palampore; Indian calico, 17th-18th century. Collection Braquenie, Paris" from which I made the wash drawing on page 182. All the bizarre elements are here: the slightly obscene shapes, the improbable flowers. Except for its somewhat static quality, I would have been satisfied, at this point, that the people who made such a highly-decorative cotton hanging could also have produced the brocade damasks we are discussing. But Slomann's evidence becomes over-abundant. It piles up—from every quarter—and topples over. While I am not an authority on weaving techniques or materials available at the end of the seventeenth century (and find his picture of world economy very confusing), I feel that the decorative sources Slomann accumulates fail to add up to the class of fabrics he found a name for. What is missing? Is it sophistication?

John Irwin, Keeper of the Indian Section at the Victoria & Albert Museum, describes the crafts in India as hut industry. This may not have been the exact situation several centuries ago, but if there were factories corresponding to the royal *tiraz* or weaving ateliers in Persia, Sicily, and Spain, it seems odd that they wove a special type of pattern over a period of about fifteen years and no longer. Peter Thornton, also of the Victoria & Albert, in his lavish and meticulous *Baroque and Rococo Silks*, explains their brief existence by the whim of fashion, thus placing their manufacture, for all practical purposes, in Europe. The round trip to India and back, from western Europe, could take two years if the prevailing monsoon winds were missed. A new and elaborately-produced type of pattern, on which East and West collaborated—as they were doing on most merchandise by the eighteenth century—could hardly have been developed in such a short space of time. Also, if such goods *had* been made in India they would have left some traces of their peculiar style, and Dr. Slomann finds none. All the evidence he adduces is either from an earlier date or is contemporary. We appreciate the affinity of Bizarre silks with the flora in ancient Ajunta frescos and with what an erudite friend of mine half-facetiously calls "the beefsteak blossoms on Indian bedspreads." But other quite dissimilar shapes and—above all—a mastery of repeat are equally evident in the Bizarre silks, and of these there is, in India, no aftermath.

Elsewhere the possible prototypes and successors abound. Take the mirror from the British Iron Age, first century A.D. I would say it anticipates both Bizarre and Art Nouveau patterns. The Surrealists, you may recall, discovered their "ancestors" everywhere. They exuberantly elected Caligula, Hieronymous Bosch, Galileo, and the Marx Brothers to their pantheon without so much as "by your leave—." As to "heirs" in the arts, they are never lacking, either. Sometimes we are conscious of our inheritance, sometimes not (for it may be circuitously handed down). Jean Pillement must surely have been familiar with the fantasies that preceded him, but I doubt if many of our modern organic-abstractionists —beginning with hints thrown out by Marcel Duchamp, André Masson, and Arshile Gorky—know how bizarre they really are.

This much Dr. Slomann's research does make certain: the silks that can truly be labelled "Bizarre" are fewer in number than might be supposed (I would guess that fewer than a hundred pieces have been found) and all of them show a marked, although not easily defined, orientalism. To begin with, nothing could be less classical, less like a Renaissance pattern, than a typical Bizarre example. Where a fifteenth- or sixteenth-century European pattern might be balanced around a central core or consist of interlocking floral sprigs, a Bizarre silk, dating from the first

years of the eighteenth century, always flouts neatness and symmetry. The few writers on the subject are in agreement about this, noting that strong diagonals and long serpentine lines occur frequently. Both effects result from using lop-sided motifs, in some instances crowding them to form slanting stripes, in others, throwing the weight of the motifs alternately from right to left. Of themselves, these undulant curves are not particularly oriental. Long before the eighteenth century they played such a prominent part in decorative design that many people think of them as Gothic. It would be just as correct to think of them as Turkish. Beyond doubt, every style partakes of many styles that preceded it; yet, if it is a style, at some point it can be recognized as such. I am sure Peter Thornton (whose book made me aware of them) rightly points out that Bizarre patterns had their beginnings, as a discernable style, about a decade prior to the peak they reached around 1705, and continued on, fitfully, after they fell out of fashion a scant five years later. But I believe he and others are mistaken in supposing that three or four countries may have produced silks of equal strangeness.

Both Slomann and Thornton confuse matters by showing patterns that lie on the borderline. There is nothing very bizarre about the filagree, often symmetrical, "lace" patterns Dr. Slomann would relate to the subject, nor do I see any real exoticism in the sketches James Leman made for his father, an English weaver at Spitalfields. They are most attractive, and of the proper date (1706 to 1718—no actual fabrics made from the sketches have been found) but to my eyes look like ultra-stylized chintzes incorporating bits of chinoiserie. Mr. Thornton feels that they belong to a "Bizarre Phase," yet expresses the belief, in a footnote on page 100, that "many of the finest Bizarre silks are in fact French." This he modifies by continuing, "It is possible, however, that some of the more extreme examples were made elsewhere, perhaps in Italy where the designers were probably less inhibited than their French counterparts by the kind of classicizing that pervaded French art and taste in general at this time."

Why, one wonders, did scholars ever entertain the notion that Bizarre silks—or "the more extreme examples," if you will—were ever made anywhere except in Italy? This is substantially what Marion P. Bolles said

BORDER-LINE BIZARRES. Facing page top: BROCADE CRADLE COVER. English. 18th century. Spitalfields. (Courtesy, Museum of Fine Arts, Boston.) Bottom: SILK. Damasked and brocaded in gold. Called "Indian Pattern, about 1700" by Slomann. (The Victoria & Albert Museum, London.) Right: Detail of LACE-PATTERNED SILK. Lyons, France. Ca. 1700. (Museum für Kunsthandwerk, Dresden.) The pattern at the top is lovely and quite strange, with balustrades made of "vegetables" and falling streams of figured "water," but much too floral to be truly Bizarre. The pattern at the bottom qualifies better, although here, too, the subject seems to be "flowers," albeit they are composed of many abstract elements. So-called "lace" patterns, as at the right, do not strike me as at all bizarre, unless every pattern that has oddly shaped, diapered compartments falls in the category.

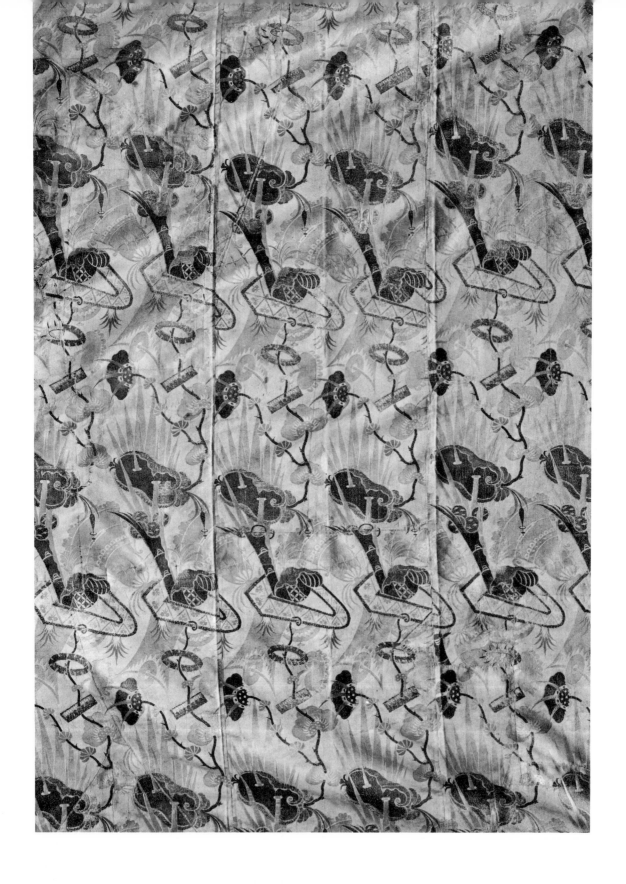

BIZARRE AT ITS BEST. Above: PIECE, WOVEN SILK AND METAL THREAD. Italian. 1705-10. Facing page: SILK, DAMASKED AND BROCADED. (Both fabrics: The Metropolitan Museum of Art. Rogers Fund, 1920.) Both are called an "Indian pattern; about 1700" by Slomann. We feel tempted to invent the motifs missing from the curious pattern, facing, of which we have only a pyramid, a turtle (?), and some shoots. But the pattern above is marvelously complete, if poorly matched. It could have been designed by Hieronymus Bosch.

in a Bulletin article, "Old Venetian Brocades," published by The Metropolitan Museum of Art in 1944, although German scholars, like Ernst Flemming, thought Spain the likely provenance. Then Slomann came along and the round of attributions may have begun all over again. On the basis of fantastic patterns woven at Lucca in the fourteenth century, I submit that the Italians had an excellent head start; yet even this argument counts less, to a designer, than the conviction that all patterns of one type must have been woven in one place.

Was this place Venice? It could have been; they had been exposed, there, to the East and to Byzantium for a long time. That could explain why the better integrated, the more "extreme" Bizarre patterns, do not give a too obviously oriental impression. They are densely covered, like so many Eastern and Near Eastern surfaces, but the sense of improvisation, so striking in Indian designs, is wholly lacking; what I called sophistication has transformed, beyond description, what were possibly once-recognizable shapes. If one wants to refer to them, words like "spiked," "perforated," "spiralling" must be used; a morbid kind of vegetation is indicated, but so are cruel mechanisms. The most typical occurrence in a truly Bizarre design is one indescribable thing growing out of another. What makes them so exquisite—for they are—is that each part functions perfectly, in its own terms, as sheer decoration.

Could such marvels have been conceived almost simultaneously in several countries and then been abandoned by all? I doubt it. The impulse behind the Bizarres was as singular and strong as that which created Cubism. As with Cubism, many elements entered into the style, but I believe only one group of artist-artisans elevated it, for a brief period, to its full intensity. What brought them together, what dispersed them and so widely distributed their work—which then, and only then, could have been modified by national tastes—may always remain a mystery. When Vilhelm Slomann, back in Copenhagen, in 1935, had gathered together so many pieces of Bizarre silk, it is a pity he did not classify them according to the abstractness of their shapes and the size and methods of their repeats, among other things. Photographs suggest the theory of a single Italian origin for the more strangely spectacular patterns—the kind that were given as gifts to synagogues—but only Slomann had the opportunity to make the necessary physical comparisons. And his heart was set on India.

A PRECURSOR AND A ECHO. Facing page top: APPLIQUED MATERIAL. France or Germany. Probably the nineteen twenties. Bottom: THE DESBOROUGH MIRROR. British Iron Age. First century. (The British Museum, London.) The "echo," top, was doubtless inspired by Cubism and Futurism, and it is interesting to note how the visual grammar of these two styles combine to produce such a Bizarre 18th-century effect. The two-thousand-year-old mirror at the bottom of the page is pure enigma. Beardsley might have given it to one of his heroines.

where and when?
——A Picture Quiz

This is a game.

Any number can play it, any number do, and have been playing some version of it most of their lives. The game consists of identifying an object. With small boys it's apt to be automobiles or aircraft, with older persons it could be birds or wines. I, myself, have been in the habit of trying to assign the artist's name to any picture that caught my eye. It must have begun in grammar school when, every year, we paid a dime to file past an exhibit of reproductions of "famous masterpieces" which had been hung around the walls and across the stage of the school auditorium —I believe on a clothesline. I always made the tour several times. They were all there, the Mona Lisa, the Laughing Cavalier, the Old Woman Paring Her Nails, the Madonna of the Chair, the Horse Fair, the Blue Boy. This game—or exercise—became still more fascinating when I was introduced to modern art by Arthur Jerome Eddy's *Cubism and Post-Impressionism* during my first year in High School. I was about thirteen years old at the time, and to tell Fauvism from Futurism seemed an important thing to do. But after a long exposure to one ism after another, the game palled a bit. Then I hit on the idea of assigning an *alternate* name to a given picture; not the name of the artist who had painted it, but that of another artist whose point of view or use of pigment, etc., suggested some affinity. Thus, seeing a particularly slick Dali I would murmur "Maxfield Parrish," or ascribe a dark, thickish Rembrandt to "Dubuffet." The more far-out the connection the better it pleased me, provided it was valid. Several gallery-going friends learned to play it this way.

The version of the game that follows may not need any such complications. To name the time and place a pattern was made, or the people who made it, may be difficult enough. A few patterns in each of my somewhat loose classifications will undoubtedly be partially identified at once, by their specific motifs or subjects. Others will be baffling because of almost unlimited probabilities: they share their character with patterns produced at a vast distance, perhaps in another era. I was prepared to find many such patterns—with continents and centuries between them—looking very much alike; I was less prepared to find patterns from a single time and place looking not at all alike. That is, it didn't surprise me to find that the Mayans and the medieval Persians used the swastika, architecturally, in similar ways; what surprised me was to see a wide variety of printed patterns issuing from a single factory in eighteenth-century France. This circumstance would not cause a raised eyebrow today; it would be called eclecticism. But it removes the general run of contemporary merchandise from our consideration since there is no point in trying to identify copies of copies. An exception has been made where the modern copy faithfully follows an original whose deteriorated condition would either betray its age or perhaps make the identification of the pattern impossible.

In every sense this is a guessing game. Students of pattern are largely dependent upon textiles; yet—we are told—textiles are not to be depended upon. As I understand the historical situation, relatively few ancient fabrics can be dated, and the place where they were found is not necessarily the place where they were made. Outstanding exceptions would be pieces of woven material with a name or an insignia that could be checked. Regarding the majority of extremely old textiles, guesswork, therefore, is inevitable and attributions prior to the sixth or seventh century are seldom seriously disputed, give or take a few centuries.

The great no-man's land of ownership begins with the Middle Ages and continues through the Renaissance. As the evidence increases, century by century, so does the apparent difficulty in identifying many of the patterns. Now and then a work of art such as a portrait of a historical person seems to pinpoint a pattern in time, but doubts are immediately raised as to where the material came from and where the pattern itself originated. These doubts are occupational with art historians, and understandably so; the game of attribution we can play so lightly is pivotal to their careers. What perplexes a non-scholar is the aura of vagueness that persisted until almost the nineteenth century, when manufacturing records were easily accessible. Perhaps new techniques of fiber and dye analysis and greater knowledge of weaving methods, from country to country, will put all "attributions" on a firmer basis. Or perhaps—and this would be my own solution—it would help if more people looked at more patterns more carefully. The pages that follow are a beginning. Identifications are on pages 224-225.

Clues to several of the patterns on the following pages have appeared in the book, but there are one or two that may surprise almost everyone. That is the pleasant thing about pattern. The more you know, the more you want to know.

1

GEOMETRICS. Above: PRINTED COTTON. Finland. 1966. (Photograph courtesy of Design Research, Cambridge, Massachusetts.) Whether or not decoration preceded illustration, pattern design began with the repetition of geometrical motifs. In its more basic forms, this type of ornamentation is so universal that it must be identified by its materials. Then, as geometric patterns become complex, it is a question of recognizing the special sensibility of a period and/or place.

2

3

195

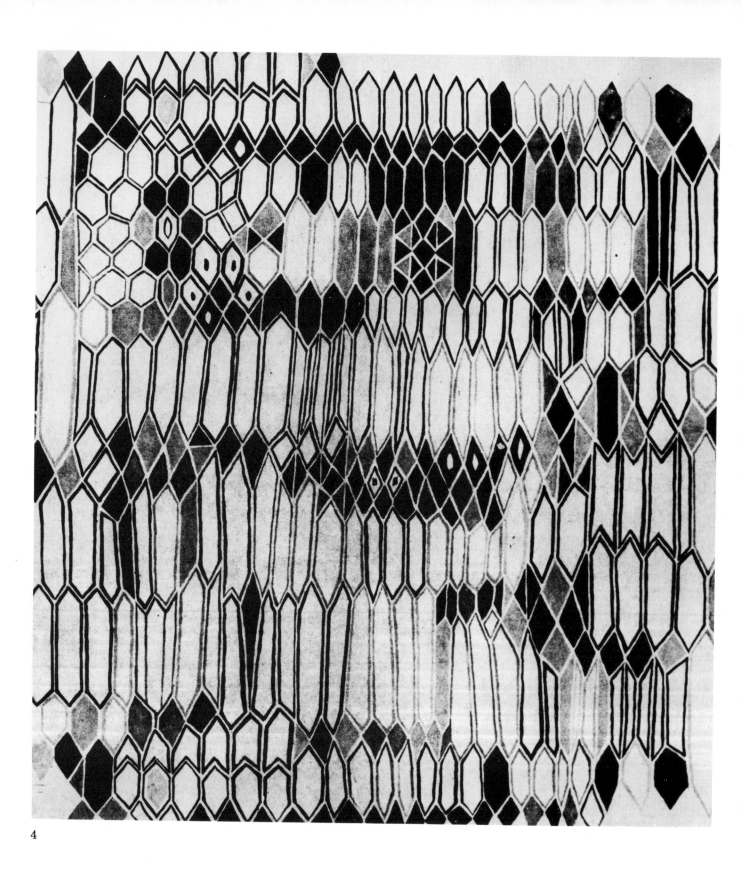

4

196

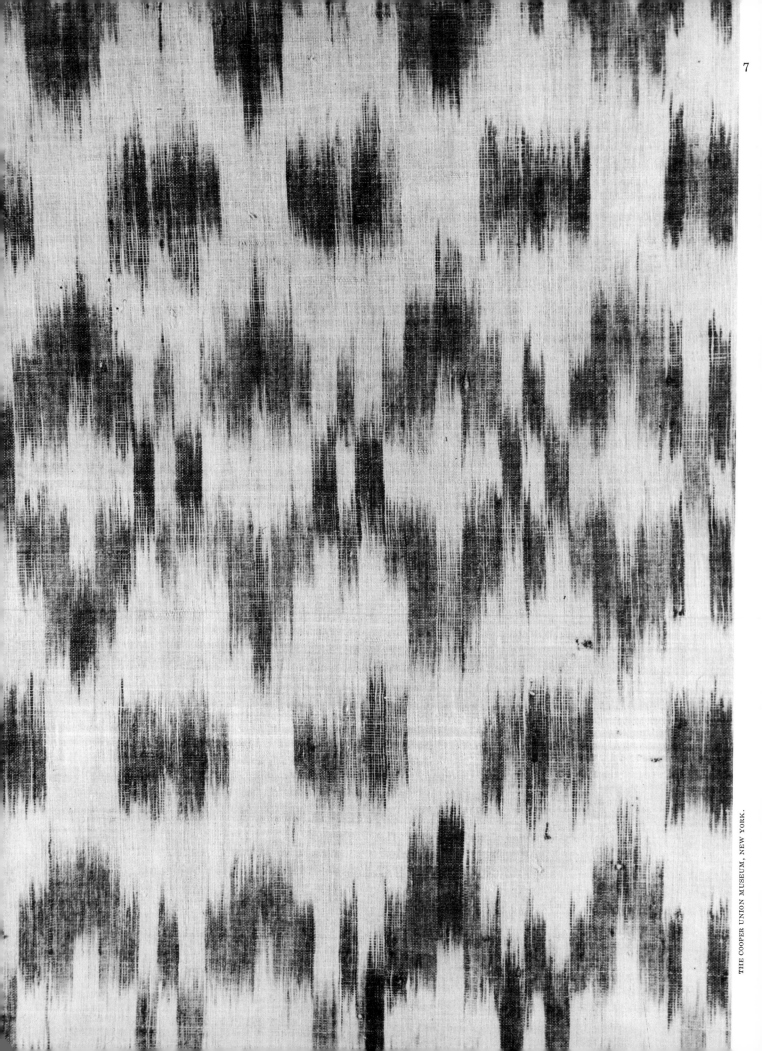

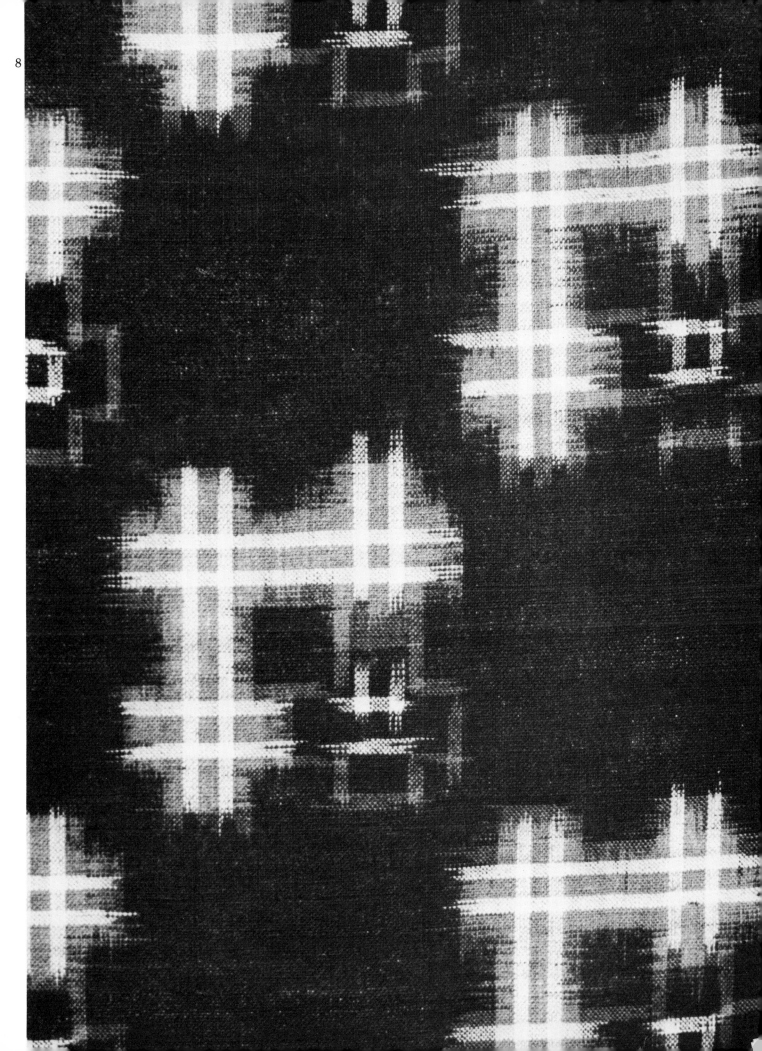

ANIMALS. Above: Brocaded Silk. Probably Italian. 14th century. (Courtesy, Museum of Fine Arts, Boston.) Animals figured in the Chinese silks of the first century B.C. Han Dynasty, but it is hard to get a good look at animal patterns much before the 6th century, in Egypt and Syria. Thereafter, throughout the Middle Ages, either their manner of presentation, or other subject matter, too easily gives them away. Consequently our patterns are fairly recent and, while few in number, cover a wide range.

18

FLORALS. Above: THEATRICAL "NOH" ROBE. Japanese. (The Philadelphia Museum of Art.) Flowers have been the chief subject of the majority of manufactured patterns for the past several hundred years. Like flower paintings, floral patterns are usually a direct expression of their times. But not always. By treating flowers in a borrowed style, it is relatively easy to make them seem to belong to any era the designer chooses.

20

21

22

23

24

THE COOPER UNION MUSEUM, NEW YORK.

25

26

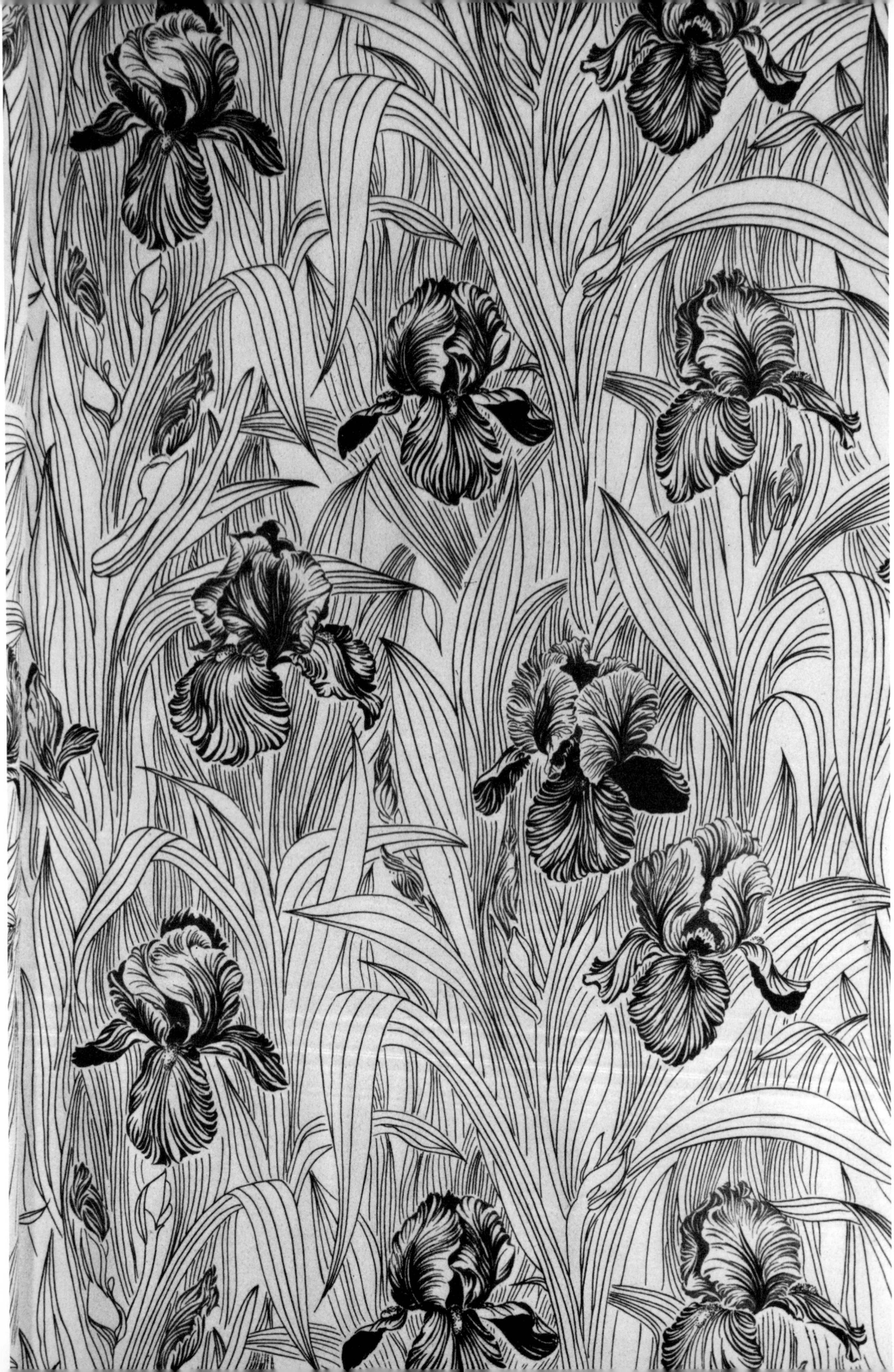

27

28

SCENICS. Above: CAPTAIN COOK'S VOYAGE. Copperplate print. England. Ca. 1780. (In the Brooklyn Museum Collection.) Scenic subjects are blatantly historical. No matter how "imaginary" the landscape—and most of them are idyllic—a designer sees it through his own period window. One of the questions about the following pictures is: which, if any, is a toile de Jouy?

29

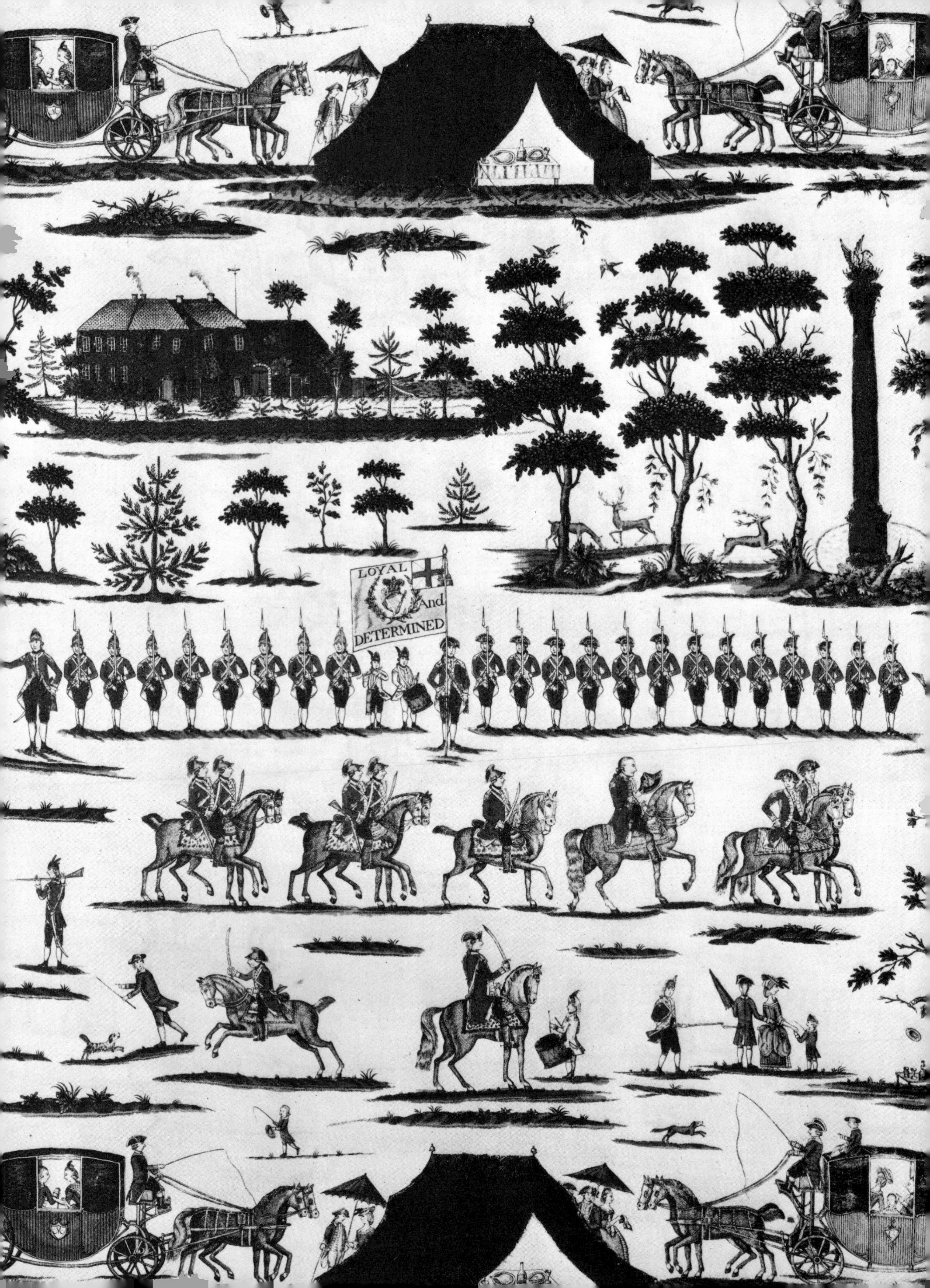
LOYAL
And
DETERMINED

30

THE DETROIT INSTITUTE OF ARTS.

216

31

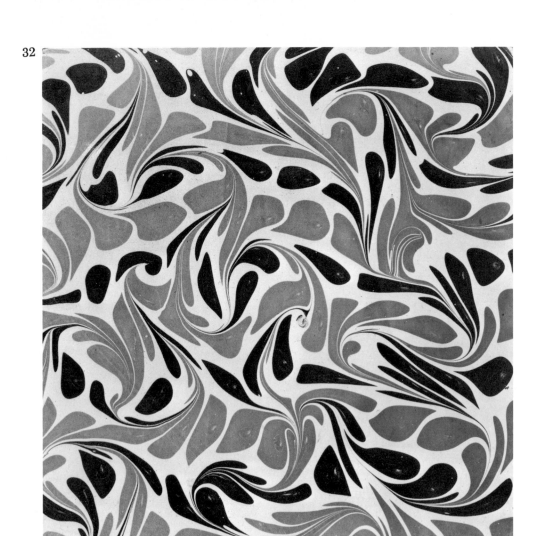

ENIGMAS. Above: Bookpaper. Experiment by William Chapman of Douglas Cockerell and Son, Cambridge, England. 1965. Who would have expected marbelizing to be so "mod"?

34

identifications

GEOMETRICS

1. Finland. 1966. PRINTED COTTON by Marimekko. (Courtesy Design Research, Cambridge, Massachusetts.)
2. Peru. Possibly Nazca Period. A combination of several weaves in what is thought to be a breechcloth. (The Textile Museum, Washington, D. C.)
3. Japan. Early 19th century. PAPER STENCIL for patterns. (The Metropolitan Museum of Art, New York.)
4. United States. Late 20th century. HEXAGONS. Pattern design by Ilonka Karasz. (Courtesy of the artist.)
5. France. Ca. 1780. WALLPAPER PRINTED FROM WOOD BLOCKS. GRISAILLE. (The Cooper Union Museum, New York. Gift of the Misses Hewitt.)
6. France, Lyons. Ca. 1925. SILK AND METAL CUT VOIDED PLAIN COMPOUND CLOTH VELVET. (The Cooper Union Museum, New York.)
7. Spain, Majorca. Late 18th century. Ikat resist dyed linen and cotton cloth. (The Cooper Union Museum, New York.)
8. Japan. End of the Edo Period. COTTON KASURI. Double ikat type. (Courtesy Sango Kogei Shikenjo.)
9. Japan. Late Edo Period. NOH ROBE. Atsu-ita weave. (Courtesy Marubeni-Iida Ltd.)
10. United States. 1890. PATCHWORK QUILT. Detail. (The Philadelphia Museum of Art.)
11. Japan. Late Edo Period. COTTON KASURI, double ikat type. (Courtesy Kurume Municipal Office, Kurume City.)

ANIMALS

12. Italy. 14th century. BROCADED SILK. (Courtesy, Museum of Fine Arts, Boston.)
13. Borneo. 19th century. BATIK PRINTED COTTON. (The Metropolitan Museum of Art. Rogers Fund.)
14. United States. Ca. 1945. THE FARM. Printed fabric designed by James Reynolds for Kent-Bragaline, Inc., New York.
15. United States. 1964. FARFALLE. Printed velvet designed by Harvey Smith for Patterson Fabrics, Inc., New York.
16. Japan. Late Edo Period. Dyework over stencilled resist on cotton. (Courtesy Mr. Fukuyo Matsubara.)
17. Spain. 17th century. DAMASK. (Courtesy, Museum of Fine Arts, Boston. Elizabeth Day McCormick Collection.)

FLORALS

18. Japan. Late 17th or early 18th century. NOH ROBE. (The Philadelphia Museum of Art.)
19. England. Ca. 1880. NAGASAKI. Silk damask designed by Bruce J. Talbert for Warner & Sons. (The Victoria & Albert Museum, London.)
20. France. Contemporary. AMANDA. Printed cotton based on botanical drawings. Imported by Brunschwig & Fils, New York.
21. United States. Contemporary reproduction of an 18th century French document. ROSES ET RUBANS. Brunschwig & Fils.
22. England. Ca. 1890. ROLLER-PRINTED COTTON. Designed by Arthur Wilcox. (The Cooper Union Museum, New York. Gift of Mr. and Mrs. G. Glen Gould.)
23. England. 1831. ROLLER-PRINTED COTTON. (The Victoria & Albert Museum, London.)
24. France. Early 19th century. PRINTED COTTON. (The Cooper Union Museum, New York.)
25. Spain. 17th century. LINEN AND WOOL DOUBLE-CLOTH. (The Cooper Union Museum, New York. Gift of J. Pierpont Morgan.)
26. United States. Contemporary printed fabric. IRIS. Elenhank Designers, Riverside, Illinois.
27. United States. Contemporary handscreened fabric and wallpaper pattern. VICTORIA. Leoda da Mar.

SCENICS

28. England. Ca. 1780. CAPTAIN COOK'S VOYAGE. Copperplate print. (In the Brooklyn Museum Collection.)
29. Ireland. 1782. LORD CHARLEMANT REVIEWING THE VOLUNTEERS IN PHOENIX PARK, DUBLIN. Copperplate print. (Courtesy, Museum of Fine Arts, Boston.)
30. Italy, Venice. 18th century textile. SHIPS AT SEA. (Courtesy of the Detroit Institute of Arts.)
31. Italy or France. Ca. 1708. BROCADED DAMASK. (Courtesy, Museum of Fine Arts, Boston, Textile Income Purchase Fund.)

ENIGMAS

32. England. Contemporary experimental BOOK PAPER. William Chapman of Douglas Cockrell and Son, Cambridge, England.
33. India. 20th century. APPLIQUED CLOTH. (The Philadelphia Museum of Art.)
34. Italy. 19th century. BOOK PAPER. (Collection of Olga Hirsh, Cambridge, England.)
35. Japan. 18th century. WOVEN SILK AND METAL THREADS. (The Metropolitan Museum of Art. Rogers Fund.)
36. England. Contemporary wallcovering. PARTI. The Wall Paper Manufacturers Limited, London.
37. Turkey. 16th century. CHILD'S TUNIC. Silk and gold brocade. (The Victoria & Albert Museum, London.)

some useful distinctions

There is no glossary because all the words used in this book can be found in most dictionaries or are defined on the spot. Only the word "pattern" might be distinguished, more emphatically, from the two words that share some of its characteristics: "design" and "ornament." That is, a pattern may be loosely referred to as a design, but not all designs are patterns. Where the word design is used alone it generally refers to a separate composition—not to a continuous all-over embellishing for which the proper word is pattern. Ornament is another term which is often used loosely. While "ornamentation" might apply to many forms of decoration, an ornament is a decorative motif which is usually complete in itself. Thus in describing a Persian carpet one might speak of a large *design* which has a *pattern* in the background, and compartment or medallion *ornaments* in the foreground. With these distinctions in mind, there is no harm in referring to an area as being "patterned"—provided the decorative elements are well distributed. Patterning, in brief, is a question of the total effect, and is not confined to instances of mechanical repetition.

a special note of thanks

I want to express my gratitude to a number of persons who gave me encouragement, information, and advice, trusting I may do so on an individual rather than an official basis—since some of my conclusions are controversial. In the order I appealed to them and they graciously responded, I am indebted to the following:

Mr. Hans J. Dorfer. Mr. Jean Koefoed. Mr. William E. Katzenbach. Miss Eleanor Le Maire. Mr. John Maxon. Mr. T. H. Robsjohn-Gibbings. Mr. Ross E. Taggart. Mr. Laurence Sickman. Miss Alice B. Beer. Miss Edith Adams. Mr. A. Burton Carnes. Mr. Joseph R. Dunlap. Mr. R. C. H. Briggs. Miss Daphne Sanderson. Mrs. Barbara J. Morris. Mr. John Irwin. Mr. Peter K. Thornton. Mr. John Beckwith. Miss Jean Mailey. Mrs. Sidney Hart. Marchese Emilio Pucci. Dr. Richard P. Wunder. Mr. James Seeman. Miss Petronel Lukens. Mr. Charles Grant Ellis. Mr. Milton Sonday. Dr. Priscilla E. Muller. Mrs. Florence Lewis May. Mrs. Alice Wilson Frothingham. Miss Daphne Hoffman. Mr. Thurman Rotan. Mr. Franco Scalamandré. Miss Rita Battistini. Mr. Alfonso Ossorio. Miss Pearl Moeller. Mr. Richard Tooke. Mrs. Zelina Brunschwig. Miss Joan Kaminsky. Mrs. Murray Douglas. Mr. Calvin Hathaway. Mr. S. Nakajima. Miss Dassah Saulpaugh. Miss Dorothy Tricarico. Miss Ilonka Karasz. Miss Mary E. Dunn. Mr. Edward A. Bragaline. Mr. Ben Piazza. Mr. Carmen D'Avino. Mr. John Eliot Alden. Mr. Adolph Cavallo. Mrs. June Kenyon. Mr. B. H. Hellman. Mr. and Mrs. Ned O. Yang. Mrs. Alba Lorman. Mr. Lou Tschopp. Miss Maria Leiper. Mrs. Lee Graham. Mr. Jimmy Ernst.

BIBLIOGRAPHY

foreword

Barr, Jr., Alfred H. *Picasso, Fifty Years of His Art.* New York: The Museum of Modern Art, 1946; Arno Press, 1966.

————. *Matisse, His Art and His Public.* New York: The Museum of Modern Art, 1951; Arno Press, 1966.

These are surely the definitive works on their subjects, indispensable for reference and stimulation. Although they do not complete the creative span of either artist, they make clear that Picasso and Matisse, between them, anticipated the major styles of twentieth-century art. The early date of some of the pictures is incredible. Both books are being revised.

————, Editor. *Fantastic Art: Dada, Surrealism.* New York. The Museum of Modern Art, 1936.

An exhibition catalogue which prophetically presents what may well be a roster of "fantastic and marvelous" landmarks in European and American art over five decades. They are all here, including the fur-lined tea cup.

Grosser, Maurice. *The Painter's Eye.* New York: Rinehart, 1951; New American Library, 1956. Paperback.

An unpretentious book primarily about the craft of painting. But since the author is one of the finest painters and art critics in the United States, we share a painter's mind as well as his eye.

Malraux, André. *The Voices of Silence.* One-volume American edition. New York: Doubleday & Company, Inc., 1953.

Esthetic's last, heroic stand. Required reading because its more striking ideas should be encountered as Malraux expressed them, rhetoric and all. The illustrative material is used freshly, often to stunning effect.

Read, Herbert. *The Meaning of Art.* Third Edition. New York: Pitman Publishing Corp., 1951. Baltimore: Penguin Books, Inc., 1959. Paperback.

This rather disjointed resumé of art history, its techniques and attitudes, is nonetheless a good general introduction to the subject.

Also recommended:

Canaday, John. *Mainstreams of Modern Art.* New York: Holt, Rinehart and Winston, Inc., 1965.

Fry, Roger. *Vision and Design.* Cleveland: World Publishing Company, 1965.

Kuh, Katherine. *Break-up: The Core of Modern Art.* New York Graphic Society, 1965.

Lippard, Lucy R. and others. *Pop Art.* New York: Frederick A. Praeger, Inc., 1967.

part 1 the nature of pattern

Pattern in general

Erdmann, Kurt. *Oriental Carpets.* Translated by Charles Grant Ellis. American edition. New York: Universe Books, Inc., 1960.

Included under "pattern in general" because, in a text of less than fifty pages, it displays more knowledge of pattern, as a distinct art form, than can be found in a dozen average books on ornament or design.

Evans, Joan. *Pattern, A Study of Ornament in Western Europe from 1180 to 1900.* Two volumes. New York: Oxford University Press, 1931.

The title is misleading. Like the several books listed below, this is mostly concerned with individual design motifs whose development it traces in a scholarly way, although with considerable sentiment. Fine for leisurely perusal.

Hamlin, A. D. F. *A History of Ornament.* New York: The Century Company. Vol. I. *Ancient and*

Medieval, 1916. Vol. II. *Renaissance and Modern*, 1923.

One could not ask for more intelligible textbooks. While they virtually omit the Far East, and are a bit repetitious, there are nearly a thousand pictures in the two volumes, all of them closely related to fact-filled texts.

Jones, Owen. *A Grammar of Ornament*. London: Bernard Quarich, 1910 and 1928. First printed in 1865.

Long considered the bible of decorative design, this imposing volume now seems a curiosity from the Victorian era.

Meyer, Franz Sales. *A Handbook of Ornament*. New York: Dover Publications Inc., 1957. Paperback. Printed in book form in Germany in 1889.

Not really a working handbook, but far more valuable than the usual grab-bag of design motifs. There were many holes in art history when this and the Jones book were produced, but an extra effort at completeness, here, yields some unexpected information.

Pattern in particular

Barrett, Douglas and Basil Gray. *Painting of India*. Cleveland: (Skira) World Publishing Company, 1963.

A source-book of stylized motifs nearly equal in character to those in *Egyptian Painting*, noted below, and — naturally — much more colorful.

Dalton, O. M. *Byzantine Art and Archeology*. New York: Oxford University Press, Inc., 1911; Dover Publications Inc., 1961. Paperback.

What would now be called a "dialogue" between East and West took one of its earliest, most substantial forms in Byzantium with the founding of "new Rome" at Constantinople in A.D. 330. This book gives a clear picture of the forces involved.

Dye, Daniel Sheets. *A Grammar of Chinese Lattice*. Cambridge, Mass.: Harvard University Press, 1949.

Over 500 line drawings make this one of the most obviously useful books a designer could have in his library. While the majority of the illustrations are taken from architectural grille-work, their application is unlimited. Used with intelligence and subtlety, "lattice" can provide the underlying structure, the repeat, for motifs of every description.

Frankfort, Henri. *The Art and Architecture of the Ancient Orient*. In the Pelican History of Art series. Baltimore: Penguin Books, Inc., 1964.

This title was selected from several contenders because it points up the relation of the Mesopotamian to the Egyptian and other civilizations "from about 3000 to 500 B. C. when Greece took the lead." The sooner one learns to distinguish between these early styles the better.

Gardner, Helen. *Art Through the Ages*. Fourth edition revised under the editorship of Sumner McK. Crosby by the Department of the History of Art, Yale University, New York: Harcourt, Brace & World, Inc., 1959.

Described as "the standard world history of art for the general reader," and certainly an excellent 840-page reference book. By keeping the hundreds of pictures relatively small, the usual coverage of European art has been extended to all of Asia, the two Americas, Africa, and Oceania, while modern art, architecture, and photography are also treated in considerable detail.

Godard, André. *The Art of Iran*. London: George Allen and Unwin, Ltd., 1965.

The emphasis is archaeological. But although architectural construction, ground plans, and ancient sculpture—especially the Luristan bronzes—are detailed almost redundantly, the illustrations are rich in unusual ornamented walls, and the various eras of Persian history and culture are presented as distinctly as seems possible.

Haemmerle, Albert. *Buntpapier*. Munich: George D. W. Callwey, 1961.

A specialized collection of patterns and designs, and one which has not as yet appeared with an English text. It should. "Bookpapers" have followed the trend of taste in every country where they were made, always adding the charm which is only found in small hand-produced decorations.

Hempel, Eberhard. *Baroque Art and Architecture in Central Europe*. Baltimore: Penguin Books, 1965.

Outside of Italy, where it began, Baroque took different forms in each country, but never exhibited greater flair than in parts of Germany and Austria.

Hillier, J. *The Japanese Print*. Rutland, Vermont, and Tokyo, Japan: Charles R. Tuttle, 1960.

An eye-opener. By stressing the psychological attitudes taken towards Japanese prints, both at home and abroad, Mr. Hillier shows us our old friends in a new light. Irreverent and irresistible.

Hudson, G. F. *Europe & China*. Boston: The Beacon Press, 1931.

In the author's opinion, the best book on the subject, making most discussions of "chinoiserie" seem superficial and superfluous, how-

228

ever beguiling. Chinoiserie, in one form or another, has been a recurring phenomenon for many centuries.

Janson, H. W. *History of Art*. New York: Harry N. Abrams. Ninth printing, 1966.
"The more you know about pattern the more you want to know" and Dr. Janson's book, subtitled "A Survey of the Major Visual Arts from the Dawn of History to the Present Day," provides the firm, flexible framework to hold in place all the knowledge we may acquire. Skillful organization into fresh categories gives even the more familiar subjects an air of discovery.

Jacques, Renata and Ernst Flemming. *Encyclopedia of Textiles*. New York: Frederick A. Praeger, Inc., 1958.
Because of the abundance of exceptional illustrations—of the types of patterns a practicing designer often needs to refer to—this is a valuable book to own. But the short text is disappointing. Sharp insights into pattern and style end abruptly in generalities. Also, to be "encyclopedic," the few pages of Japanese and Peruvian textiles need to be extended beyond a sampling from Central European museums. Doubtless this will be done in a future edition.

Kuhn, Herbert. *Rock Pictures in Europe*. New York: American edition by Essential Books, 1956.
For a designer, this is worth all the coffee-table books on cave painting put together. Reduced to line illustrations, it becomes possible to judge prehistoric images on their artistic merit, without the speculation about their purported magic—which color photographs apparently encourage.

Lee, Sherman E. *A History of Far Eastern Art*. New York: Harry N. Abrams, Inc., 1964.
The Orient between two covers. Here is a long-awaited gathering together and relating of all the great periods of art throughout the Far East. With this book by Dr. Lee, and H. W. Janson's *History of Art*—which stresses the Occident—a student would have a firm foundation for an art library.

Lichten, Frances. *Decorative Art of Victoria's Era*. New York: Charles Scribner's Sons. 1950.
An extremely amusing book about a quite unbelievable time. The author's ambivalence towards her subject matter is rather disconcerting—for she seems in sympathy with much that she holds up to ridicule—but, judging from her photograph on page 252, she may have been uncomfortably close to what she describes.

Mekhitarian, Arpag. *Egyptian Painting*. Cleveland: (Skira) World Publishing Company, 1954.
All the Skira books are rewarding, at least pictorially, but this volume is of special interest to anyone searching for pattern inspiration. The Egyptian mural painters used flat shapes and few colors to make some of the most vivid images in the world. Commonplace subjects have never been treated more expressively.

Morey, Charles Rufus. *Medieval Art*. New York: W. W. Norton, Inc., 1942.
Beginning with "the dissolution of classic style in early Christian art," ca. 300, Dr. Morey's study covers the Byzantine and Romanesque periods to "High" and late Gothic, ca. 1450. The advantage of this long span is that it shows the art of the Middle Ages as an outgrowth of the Greco-Roman tradition, much transformed by the Orient, with its mysticism largely supplied by the Celtic-Teutonic "barbarians" from the west and north. Thus framed, Gothic naturalism becomes doubly pleasing. Splendid, instructive line drawings. (NOTE: The decorative side of the Renaissance is amply covered in the books on textiles and art history, listed above, and further on.)

Pope, Arthur Upham. *Masterpieces of Persian Art*. New York: The Dryden Press, 1945.
In effect, Dr. Pope's renowned six-volume *A Survey of Persian Art* in capsule form. Ravishing pictures.

Rheims, Maurice. *The Flowering of Art Nouveau*. New York: Harry N. Abrams, Inc., 1966.
Wild and wonderful. Viewed so comprehensively—from its architecture, furnishings, and jewelry, to its graphics and "funerary art"—the brief Art Nouveau period emerges as a serious, if somewhat strenuous, effort to create an original style.

Sardo, Enrique. Photographs by Wim Swaan. *Moorish Spain*. London: Elek Books, 1963.
More penetrating than it first appears to be, what with so many handsome illustrations. The principal Andalusian cities—Cordoba, Sevilla, Granada—are treated separately, to bring out the special qualities of their monuments, but above all else the whole eight hundred years of Islamic occupation is set forth with exceptional clarity.

Sitwell, Sacheverill. *Southern Baroque Art*. Third edition. London: Duckworth, 1963.
Subtitled "A Study of painting, architecture and music," this is possibly Mr. Sitwell's masterpiece, a poet's distillation of the most emotion-fraught style ever conceived.

Strzygowski, Josef. *Origin of Christian Church Art*.

New York: Oxford University Press, 1923.
A formidable book by a great and passionate scholar. Should be read as an intellectual adventure story.

Textile Color Design Center. *Textile Designs of Japan*. Three volumes. Japan, Osaka: 1959-61.
It is impossible to imagine a more impressive demonstration of sheer designing ability—on the part of a single nation, over a period of less than three hundred years. These books prove conclusively that the Japanese possess boundless imagination and impeccable taste, and that whether they invent or appropriate the motifs they use scarcely matters.

Thornton, Peter. *Baroque and Rococo Silks*. London: Faber and Faber, 1965.
A volume that sets new standards of unpedantic thoroughness, both in its text and the selection of pictures. Aside from the assumption—shared by so many—that textile design reached its zenith with the naturalistic, painterly designs of Jean Revel and Philippe de Lasalle, Mr. Thornton shows a keen appreciation of pattern. And his lively sense of history makes capital reading.

Weibel, Adèle Coulin. *Two Thousand Years of Textiles*. New York: Pantheon Books Inc., 1952.
The principal omnibus book on the subject in English. Short sections on the materials and techniques of weaving precede a general history of woven fabrics up to the nineteenth century. Except for the complete exclusion of the Far East and Peru, this is such an informative work that it is a pity the illustrations—all from North American collections—and their descriptions are separated as they are. Economical, perhaps, but very awkward.

Weltfish, Gene. *The Origins of Art*. Indianapolis, Ind.: Bobbs-Merrill Company, Inc., 1952.
A lucid and detailed account of the theory that most design motifs originate in such "industries" as mat-weaving or skin-working. Fascinating, although—to the author—unconvincing.

Wessel, Klaus. *Coptic Art in Early Christianity*. New York: McGraw-Hill Book Company, 1965.
Egyptian Christendom as a depot of artistic ideas. While Coptic art can be amusingly called "Greek Provincial," it brought together decorative material which eventually found its way throughout Europe.

Also recommended:

Boas, Franz. *Primitive Art*. New York: Dover Publications Inc., 1955. Paperback.

Durant, Will. *Our Oriental Heritage*. Vol. I of *The Story of Civilization*. New York: Simon and Schuster, Inc., 1935.

Goodyear, William H. *The Grammar of the Lotus*. London: Sampson Low, Marston and Co., 1891.

Honour, Hugh. *Chinoiserie, The Vision of Cathay*. New York: E. P. Dutton & Company, 1961.

Jourdain, Margaret and R. Soame Jenyns. *Chinese Export Art*. New York: Charles Scribner's Sons, 1950.

Linton, Ralph and Paul S. Wingert. *Arts of the South Seas*. New York: The Museum of Modern Art, 1946.

May, Florence Lewis. *Silk Textiles of Spain: Eighth to Fifteenth Century*. New York: The Hispanic Society of America, 1957.

Marinotos, Spyridon. Photographs by Max Hirmer. *Crete and Mycenae, The Glories and Art Heritage of Early Grecian Cultures*. New York: Harry N. Abrams, Inc., 1960.

Parrot, André. *Sumner, The Dawn of Art*. New York: Golden Press, 1961.

Pope, Arthur Upham, Editor. *A Survey of Persian Art From Prehistoric Times to the Present*. Thirteen volumes and an Index. New York: Oxford University Press, 1965. First issued in six volumes, 1938-39.

Santangelo, Antonino. *Italian Silk Design From the 12th to the 18th Century*. London: A. Zwemmer, 1964.

Von Falke, Otto. *Decorative Silks*. Third edition. New York: William Helbrun, 1936.

pARt ii pAttERN mAkiNG

Line

Best-Maugard, Adolfo. *A Method for Creative Design*. New York: Alfred A. Knopf, Inc., 1926.
Listed here because the method is predominantly linear. Whether it would lend itself to large-scale decoration is questionable, but its suitability for small areas has been proven by two generations of teachers and students. The "method" is the result of an inspired study of Mexican folk art, and the book is still in print after forty years.

Chiang, Yee. *Chinese Calligraphy*. Cambridge, Mass.: Harvard University Press, 1954.
The heart of the matter. A graphic demonstration of the sheer power and character—in the smallest brushstroke—which finally sets Chinese art apart from all the others.

Etemble. *The Written Word*. London: Prentice-Hall International, 1962.
A "line collection" in itself. The distinctions between the various types of writing and printing, and the pertinent information about each, are beautifully presented. Valuable for an understanding of calligraphic style in

general.

Steinberg, Saul. *The Catalogue*. Cleveland, Ohio: World Publishing Company, 1962.

Every designer should own at least one book by Steinberg—besides clipping the best of him from *The New Yorker*. *The Catalogue*, "A selection of drawings from *The art of living, The passport*, (and) *The labyrinth*," would be a good choice.

Also of interest:

Bosserk, Helmut Th. *Peasant Art of Europe and Asia*. New York: Frederick A. Praeger, 1959.

Shape

Graphis Press, The. *Graphis 100—The Sun*. Switzerland, Zurich: 1962.

The spectacular hundredth-anniversary number of this international journal is being reprinted. Nothing could be more instructive for the budding designer than to see how a single motif—the sun symbol—undergoes seemingly endless change in the hands of scores of famous, and anonymous, artists the world over, throughout history.

Janis, Harriet and Rudi Blesh. *Collage*. Philadelphia: Chilton Book Co., 1962.

An amazingly thorough job of putting together all the diverse material related to this pivotal art technique. Much nonsense, but not on the authors' part.

Penrose, Roland. *The Sculpture of Picasso*. Chronology by Alicia Legg. New York: The Museum of Modern Art, 1967.

Photographs fail to convey the supreme comic spirit that pervaded the exhibition covered by this book and catalogue. However, it does suggest that no other sculptor has used "found" objects quite so brilliantly, or given such variety to the human face.

Soby, James Thrall. *Juan Gris*. New York: The Museum of Modern Art, 1958.

Juan Gris is the star pupil of Cubism, the master of dove-tailing. Although there may sometimes be more impressive collections of illustrations from an artist's work, all MOMA catalogues, published at the time of each exhibition, are both informative and handsome, and are usually available hardbound and paperbound.

Also recommended:

Lieberman, William S., Editor. With an introduction. *Max Ernst*. New York: The Museum of Modern Art, 1961.

Soby, James Thrall. *Arp*. New York: The Museum of Modern Art, 1958.

————. *René Magritte*. New York: The Museum of Modern Art, 1965.

Wheeler, Monroe. *The Last Works of Henri Matisse: Large Cut Gouaches*. New York: The Museum of Modern Art, 1961.

Texture

Kepes, Gyorgy. *The New Landscape in art and science*. Chicago: Paul Theobold & Co., 1956.

The forms and patterns found in nature have long been considered a major design source, particularly as revealed by the camera close-up. Professor Kepes sees his new landscape both from farther away and infinitely nearer. Aerial photographs and laboratory photomicrographs carry the burden of his apparent conviction that, since scientific data sometimes resembles modern art, modern artists would benefit from studying it.

O'Conner, Francis V. *Jackson Pollock*. New York: The Museum of Modern Art, 1967.

Catalogue for a large retrospective show. This scrupulously documented book serves the artist better than the actual exhibit did. Here Pollock's successes can be more readily singled out and appreciated.

Richardson, John *G. Braque*. London: Oldbourne Press, 1951.

Georges Braque, the third member of the Big Three of twentieth-century art, never received the wide acclaim accorded the other two, Matisse and Picasso. This superb volume suggests why, because it shows that, unlike his peers, Braque was incapable of treating a surface casually, but always demanded qualities that made his own work appear less vigorous, even precious.

Also recommended:

Gowing, Lawrence. *Turner: Imagination and Reality*. New York: The Museum of Modern Art, 1966.

Rewald, John and others. *Odilon Redon. Gustave Moreau. Rudolphe Bresdin*. New York: The Museum of Modern Art, 1961.

Seitz, William C. *The Art of Assemblage*. New York: The Museum of Modern Art, 1961.

Selz, Peter. With texts by the artist. *The Work of Jean Dubuffet*. New York: The Museum of Modern Art, 1962.

Color

Birren, Faber. *Creative Color*. New York: Reinhold Book Corporation, 1961.

Presents the various scientific theories of color, simply, usefully, and imaginatively.

Elliot, James, James Thrall Soby, and Monroe Wheeler. *Bonnard and His Environment*. New York: The Museum of Modern Art, 1964.

The catalogue for a quite astonishing exhibition. Bonnard, as a late Impressionist master, was known to be a great colorist, but here, in one picture after another, he used the kind of off-beat color combinations that Matisse habitually explored, and which are being so zealously exploited at the present time. 107 illustrations, 41 in color.

Itten Johannes. *The Art of Color*. New York: Reinhold Book Corporation, 1961.

A serenely competent handling of a subject that can become either extremely technical or trite. All the theory any artist needs, plus student work and the analysis of how color functions in famous paintings, makes this the color book that has everything. Enjoyable reading.

Also recommended:

Chevreul, M. E. *The Principles of Harmony and Contrast of Colors*. With a special introduction and explanatory notes by Faber Birren. New York: Reinhold Book Corporation, 1967.

Mayer, Ralph. *The Artist's Handbook of Materials & Techniques*. New York: Viking Press, Inc., revised edition, 1963. Seventh printing.

General works

Christie, Archibald H. *Traditional Methods of Pattern Designing: An Introduction to the Study of Formal Ornament*. Oxford: At the Clarendon Press, 1910. Second edition, 1929.

With the Lewis Day book, listed below, the only books devoted to pattern—on an adult level—in English. This one broaches the subject historically and recognizes the importance of natural motifs, but shows confusion regarding the role of "ornament." It ends with four chapters of elaborate geometrical layouts, presumably to justify its pattern claims.

Day, Lewis F. *Pattern Design*. London: B. T. Batsford, Ltd. New York: Charles Scribner's Sons. First published in 1903, with a number of editions between 1915 and 1933, revised and enlarged by Amor Fenn.

Subtitled "A book for students, treating in a practical way of the anatomy, planning, and evolution of repeated ornament," this volume would have saved me years of struggling with structural problems had I discovered it earlier. Yet it has its hazards. Geometrical in its approach, its fails to provide a satisfactory bridge between geometry and nature—where most of our motifs come from. But practicing pattern makers who already know how to integrate motifs with structure will find this book a godsend. Well worth searching for.

De Sausmarez, Maurice. *Basic Design: The dynamics of visual form*. New York: Reinhold Book Corporation, 1964.

One of the few books on design in general that can be recommended. The material is well organized, the terminology explicit and sensible. If there is a reservation to be made it is with regard to whether serious art can be produced by sheer calculation, as the book implies.

Also of interest:

Carraher, Ronald G. and Jacqueline B. Thurston. *Optical Illusions and the Visual Arts*. New York: Reinhold Book Corporation, 1966.

Luckiesh, M. *Visual Illusions: Their Causes, Characteristics & Applications*. Introduction by William H. Ittelson. New York: Dover Publications Inc., 1965. Paperback. First published in 1922.

Seitz, William C. *The Responsive Eye*. New York: The Museum of Modern Art, 1964.

part iii aspects of pattern

New Documents for Old

Fairchild, John Burr. *The Fashionable Savages*. New York: Doubleday & Company, Inc., 1965.

An entertaining behind-the-scenes report on promotions, espionage, and the handful of truly creative persons in the fashion industry. With different casts, it could be an account of what goes on in any of the decorative arts.

Entwistle, E. A. *The Book of Wallpaper, A History and an Appreciation*. With an introduction by Sacheverill Sitwell. London: Arthur Baker, 1954.

For zealots. The curious story of wallpaper, decked out with a full complement of its horrors. Completely fascinating.

Floud, Peter. *Printed English Textiles 1720-1836*. London: The Victoria & Albert Museum, and Her Majesty's Stationery Office, 1960.

A generous picture book, compiled by Mr. Floud, with an introduction that is a marvel of concise information. Textiles were printed by machine from copper plates in Ireland, before they were in England. When machine-printing did supplant the wood block the deterioration in pattern design was rapid and unmistakable. Incidentally, the forerunners of William Morris's more naturalistic style are all here.

Katzenbach, Lois and William. *The Practical Book of American Wallpaper*. Introduction by Nancy V. McClelland. Philadelphia and New York: J. B. Lippincott Company, 1951.

Puts wallpaper's best foot forward. The firm

founded by William Katzenbach and Phelps Warren was largely responsible for the wallpaper renaissance of the thirties, in America, and this volume, illustrated with actual sheets of wallpaper, shows the standards the firm set, and the trends its started.

McClelland, Nancy V. *Historic Wallpapers From their Inception to the Introduction of Machinery*. Philadelphia and New York: J. B. Lippincott Company, 1924.

As Miss McClelland knew, wallpaper has been a major factor in the dissemination and, also, in the corruption of pattern. While her book stresses antique papers of great opulence, the pitfalls ahead are all anticipated.

The Handpainted Soapbox

Henderson, Philip. *William Morris, His Life, Work and Friends*. Foreword by Allan Temko. New York, Toronto, London, Sydney: McGraw-Hill Book Company, 1967.

There are a number of good books on Morris, but this is the first full-scale "life" that gives some of the long-withheld facts of his marriage.

Mackail, J. W. *Life of William Morris*. London: World's Classics Series, 1950. Originally published in two volumes, London, 1899.

The standard biography, which appeared three years after Morris' death. Understandably reticent on some matters, this is the book that should have told us how Morris acquired his outstanding skill, that of pattern designer. Ingratiating, nonetheless.

Also recommended:

Paul Thompson. *The Work of William Morris*. New York: The Viking Press, 1967.

Watkinson, Ray. *William Morris as Designer*. New York: Reinhold Book Corporation, 1967.

A Class By Themselves

Irwin, John. "Origins of the 'Oriental Style' in English Decorative Art." London: *The Burlington Magazine*, April 1955.

The article that reversed scholarly trade winds. Mr. Irwin's findings are central to any serious discussion of patterns and their origins, since they show, quite conclusively, that sources are not always where they appear to be.

Parr, Charles McKew. *Jan Van Linschoten the Dutch Marco Polo*. New York: Thomas Y. Crowell, 1964.

How the East-West trade in the early seventeenth century looked to, and profited, an ambitious young sailor. A factual account of the appalling hardships and persistent intrigue behind the traffic in spices, textiles, and porcelains.

Slomann, Vilhelm. *Bizarre Designs in Silks*. Translated by Calvin Hathaway. Copenhagen: Ejner Munksgaard, 1953.

A real extravaganza. Possibly the most provocative book in the field of fabrics. The translator may be right in saying Dr. Slomann's theories have not been disproved. Perhaps they cannot be. What is so exhilarating is that both the subject and the argument for its origins express a degree of fantasy only reached, briefly, at rare intervals in art history. Art Nouveau touched it. So did Surrealism.

General works

McCarthy, Mary. *The Stones of Florence*. New York: Harcourt, Brace & World, Inc., 1959.

———. *Venice Observed*. New York: Harcourt, Brace & World, Inc., 1963.

Two of the best art books of our time.

Pevsner, Nikolaus. *The Englishness of English Art*. London: Penguin Books, 1956. Paperback.

An utterly captivating small volume. The ostensible subject is English art and architecture from medieval days to the present, but most of Europe—and a large cast of wacky characters—become involved before what makes "Englishness" is finally defined.

Taylor, Francis Henry. *The Taste of Angels*. Boston: Little, Brown & Company, 1948.

An exemplary marshalling of the facts about collecting works of art from the time of the Pharoahs up to and including Napoleon. We are sadly poorer that the sequel was never finished. As far as it goes—a spirited outline of western culture.

List of Illustrations

index

239

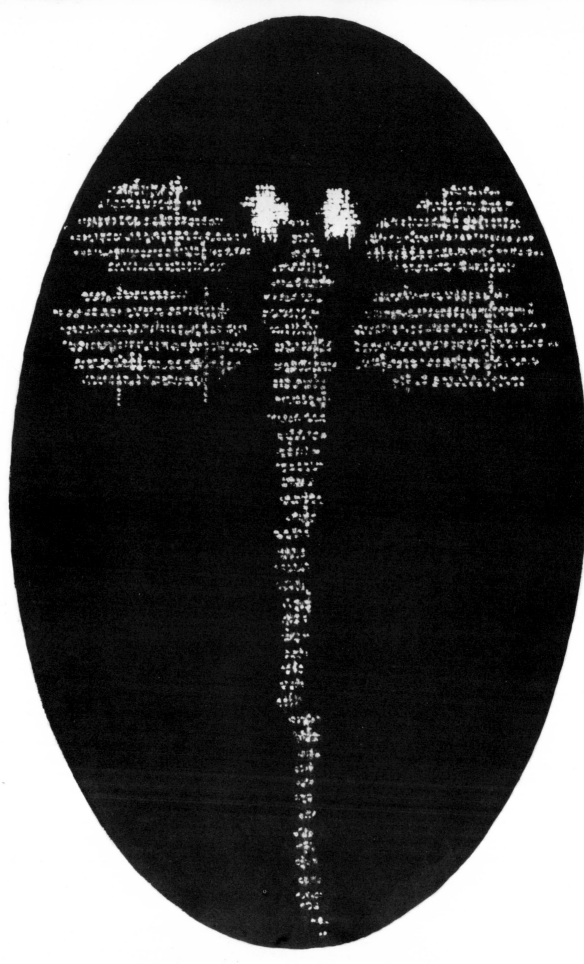

Author's sketch of a Japanese DOUBLE IKAT DRAGONFLY.